CENTENARY SELECTED POEMS

EDWIN MORGAN (1920–2010) was born in Glasgow. He served with the RAMC in the Middle East during World War II. He became lecturer in English at the University of Glasgow, where he had studied, and retired as titular Professor in 1980. He was Glasgow's first Poet Laureate and from 2004 until 2010 served as Scotland's first Makar, or National Poet. He was made an OBE in 1982 and received the Queen's Gold Medal for Poetry in 2000. *A Book of Lives* (2007) won the Scottish Arts Council Sundial Book of the Year. Carcanet has published most of his work, including his *Collected Poems, Collected Translations*, plays such as *A.D.: A Trilogy of Plays on the Life of Jesus Christ* and *The Play of Gilgamesh* and his translations of Rostand's *Cyrano de Bergerac* and Racine's *Phaedra*.

HAMISH WHYTE, poet, librarian, editor and publisher, lived for many years in Glasgow before moving to Edinburgh in 2004. His most recent collection of poems is *Things We Never Knew* (Shoestring, 2016). With Robert Crawford he edited *About Edwin Morgan* (EUP, 1990), which includes his checklist of Morgan's publications; he edited Morgan's *Nothing Not Giving Messages* (Polygon 1990) and contributed to *The International Companion to Edwin Morgan* (ASLS, 2015). He also runs Mariscat Press, which published many of Morgan's works. His memoir, *Morgan and Me*, will be published by Happenstance Press in 2020.

CARCANET CLASSICS INCLUDE

Srinivas Rayaprol, *Angular Desire: Selected Poems and Prose*
George Seferis, *Complete Poems*
Philip Terry, *Dictator*
Arthur Rimbaud, *Illuminations*, translated by John Ashbery
Jenny Lewis, *Gilgamesh Retold*
Elizabeth Jennings, *New Selected Poems*
William Carlos Williams, *Collected Poems Volume I & II*
Yves Bonnefoy, *Prose*
Charles Tomlinson, *Swimming Chenango Lake: Selected Poems*
Catullus, *The Books of Catullus*, translated by Simon Smith
Walt Whitman, *Walt Whitman Speaks: His Final Thoughts*
Jane Draycott, *Pearl*
Rebecca Elson, *A Responsibility to Awe*

Centenary Selected Poems

EDWIN
MORGAN

edited by

HAMISH WHYTE

CARCANET
CLASSICS

First published in Great Britain in 2020 by
Carcanet
Alliance House, 30 Cross Street
Manchester M2 7AQ
www.carcanet.co.uk

A CIP catalogue record for this book is
available from the British Library.

ISBN 978 1 78410 996 7

Text design by Andrew Latimer
Printed in Great Britain by SRP Ltd, Exeter, Devon

The publisher acknowledges financial
assistance from Arts Council England.

CONTENTS

The poems in this selection have been taken from the following
publications:

The Vision of Cathkin Braes and Other Poems (William MacLellan,
  1952)
Starryveldt (Eugen Gomringer Press, 1965)
gnomes (Akros Publications, 1968)
The Second Life (Edinburgh University Press, 1968)
Instamatic Poems (Ian McKelvie, 1972)
From Glasgow to Saturn (Carcanet Press, 1973)
The New Divan (Carcanet New Press, 1977)
Star Gate: Science Fiction Poems (Third Eye Centre, 1979)
Poems of Thirty Years (Carcanet New Press, 1982)
Grafts/Takes (Mariscat Press, 1983)
Sonnets from Scotland (Mariscat Press, 1984)
Selected Poems (Carcanet Press, 1985)
From the Video Box (Mariscat Press, 1986)
Themes on a Variation (Carcanet Press, 1988)
Collected Poems (Carcanet Press, 1990)
Hold Hands Among the Atoms (Mariscat Press, 1991)
Virtual and Other Realities (Carcanet Press, 1997)
Demon (Mariscat Press, 1999)
Cathures (Carcanet Press / Mariscat Press, 2002)
Love and a Life (Mariscat Press, 2003)
Tales from Baron Munchausen (Mariscat Press, 2005)
A Book of Lives (Carcanet Press, 2007)
Dreams and Other Nightmares (Mariscat Press, 2010)

I have used as template Edwin Morgan's own choice of his poems for the *New Selected Poems* which Carcanet published in 2000. In editing that and adding later poems, I have tried to provide a selection as widely representative as possible from the huge range of his work, from his first book in 1952 to his last in 2010.

I should like to thank most warmly David Kinloch, James McGonigal, Robyn Marsack and Pip Osmond for their extremely useful assistance in the compilation of this volume.

Hamish Whyte

CENTENARY SELECTED POEMS

VERSES FOR A CHRISTMAS CARD

This endyir starnacht blach and klar
As I on Cathkin-fells held fahr
A snaepuss fussball showerdown
With nezhny smirl and whirlcome rown
Upon my pollbare underlift,
And smazzled all my gays with srift:
Faroer fieldswhide frosbloom strayfling,
Froral brookrims hoartrack glassling,
Allairbelue beauheaven ablove
Avlanchbloomfondshowed brrumalljove.

O angellighthoused harbourmoon,
Glazegulfgalaxeval governoon,
Jovegal allcapellar jupiterror
And you brighdsun of venusacre,
Respour this leidyear Phoenixmas
With starphire and restorying dazz
Bejeweleavening cinderill
To liftlike pace and goodquadrille.
All men reguard, from grace our fere,
And sun on us to kind and chere.

```
      am              i
                              if
  i am                    he
        he r       o
        h     ur    t
        the re         and
        he    re    and
        he re
    a               n   d
        the r              e
  i am     r                  ife
                  i n
            s       ion and
  i                     d     i e
    am    e res    ect
    am    e res    ection
                      o           f
        the                   life
                      o           f
      m    e          n
            sur e
        the              d     i e
  i         s
            s     e t    and
  i am the   sur        d
    a   t    res    t
                      o       life
  i am  he r                  e
  i a           ct
  i       r  u      n
  i   m    e   e     t
  i             t          i e
```

```
i          s    t    and
i am th              o       th
i am    r                a
i am the   su        n
i am the s          on
i am the e    rect on        e  if
i am      re          n      t
i am       s           a           fe
i am       s    e    n    t
i     he e               d
i     t e   s     t
i        re           a  d
  a    th re           a  d
  a         s      t on      e
  a   t    re          a  d
  a   th   r        on        e
i          resurrect
                          a         life
i am               i n           life
i am      resurrection
i am the resurrection and
i am
i am the resurrection and the life
```

generation upon
generation upon
generation upon
generation upon
generation upon
generation upon
generation upon
generation upon
generation upon
generation upon
generation upon
generation upon
generation upon
generation upon
generation upon
generation upon
generation upon
generation upon
g neration upon
g neration up n
g nerat on up n
g nerat n up n
g nerat n   p n
g   erat n   p n
g   era   n   p n
g   era   n   n
g   er   n   n
g   r   n   n
g   n   n
g   n
g

STARRYVELDT

starryveldt
  slave
southvenus
  serve
SHARPEVILLE
  shove
shriekvolley
  swerve
shootvillage
  save
spoorvengeance
  stave
spadevoice
  starve
strikevault
  strive
subvert
  starve
smashverwoerd
  strive
scattervoortrekker
  starve
spadevow
  strive
sunvast
  starve
survive
  strive
SO: VAEVICTIS

SIESTA OF A HUNGARIAN SNAKE

s sz sz SZ sz SZ sz ZS zs ZS zs zs z

```
jollymerry
hollyberry
jollyberry
merryholly
happyjolly
jollyjelly
jellybelly
bellymerry
hollyheppy
jollyMolly
marryJerry
merryHarry
hoppyBarry
heppyJarry
boppyheppy
berryjorry
jorryjolly
moppyjelly
Mollymerry
Jerryjolly
bellyboppy
jorryhoppy
hollymoppy
Barrymerry
Jarryhappy
happyboppy
boppyjolly
jollymerry
merrymerry
merrymerry
merryChris
ammerryasa
Chrismerry
asMERRYCHR
YSANTHEMUM
```

OPENING THE CAGE

14 variations on 14 words

I have nothing to say and I am saying it and that is poetry.
John Cage

I have to say poetry and is that nothing and am I saying it
I am and I have poetry to say and is that nothing saying it
I am nothing and I have poetry to say and that is saying it
I that am saying poetry have nothing and it is I and to say
And I say that I am to have poetry and saying it is nothing
I am poetry and nothing and saying it is to say that I have
To have nothing is poetry and I am saying that and I say it
Poetry is saying I have nothing and I am to say that and it
Saying nothing I am poetry and I have to say that and it is
It is and I am and I have poetry saying say that to nothing
It is saying poetry to nothing and I say I have and am that
Poetry is saying I have it and I am nothing and to say that
And that nothing is poetry I am saying and I have to say it
Saying poetry is nothing and to that I say I am and have it

CHINESE CAT

p m r k g n i a o u
p m r k g n i a o
p m r k n i a o
p m r n i a o
p m r i a o
p m i a o
m i a o
m a o

What innocence? Whose guilt? What eyes? Whose breast?
Crumpled orphan, nembutal bed,
white hearse, Los Angeles,
DiMaggio! Los Angeles! Miller! Los Angeles! America!
That Death should seem the only protector –
That all arms should have faded, and the great cameras and lights
    become an inquisition and a torment –
That the many acquaintances, the autograph-hunters, the
    inflexible directors, the drive-in admirers should become
    a blur of incomprehension and pain –
That lonely Uncertainty should limp up, grinning, with
    bewildering barbiturates, and watch her undress and lie
    down and in her anguish
call for him! call for him to strengthen her with what could
    only dissolve her! A method
of dying, we are shaken, we see it. Strasberg!
Los Angeles! Olivier! Los Angeles! Others die
and yet by this death we are a little shaken, we feel it,
America.
Let no one say communication is a cantword.
They had to lift her hand from the bedside telephone.
But what she had not been able to say
perhaps she had said. 'All I had was my life.
I have no regrets, because if I made
any mistakes, I was responsible.
There is now – and there is the future.
What has happened is behind. So
it follows you around? So what?' – This
to a friend, ten days before.
And so she was responsible.
And if she was not responsible, not wholly responsible, Los Angeles?
    Los Angeles? Will it follow you around? Will the slow
    white hearse of the child of America follow you around?

THE WHITE RHINOCEROS

'Rare over most of its former range'
Webster's Third New International Dictionary

The white rhinoceros was eating phosphorous!
I came up and I shouted Oh no! No! No! –
you'll be extinct in two years! But he shook his ears
and went on snorting, knee-deep in pawpaws,
trundling his hunger, shrugged off the tick-birds,
rolled up his sleeves, kicked over an anthill,
crunched, munched, wonderful windfall,
empty dish. And gored that old beat-up tin tray
for more, it stuck on his horn,
looked up with weird crown on his horn
like a bear with a beehive, began to glow –
as leerie lair bear glows honeybrown –
but he glowed
                white and
                        bright and
the safety-catches started to click in the thickets
for more. Run, holy hide – take up your armour –
Run – white horn, tin clown, crown of rain-woods,
venerable shiner! Run, run, run!

And thunders glowing like a phantom
through the bush, beating the guns
this time, but will he always
when his only camouflage
is a world of white?

Save the vulnerable shiners.
Watch the phosphorous trappers.
Smash the poisonous dish.

ABERDEEN TRAIN

Rubbing a glistening circle
on the steamed-up window I framed
a pheasant in a field of mist.
The sun was a great red thing somewhere low,
struggling with the milky scene. In the furrows
a piece of glass winked into life,
hypnotized the silly dandy; we
hooted past him with his head cocked,
contemplating a bottle-end,
and this was the last of October,
a Chinese moment in the Mearns.

CANEDOLIA

An Off-Concrete Scotch Fantasia

oa! hoy! awe! ba! mey!

who saw?
rhu saw rum. garve saw smoo. nigg saw tain. lairg saw lagg. rigg
saw eigg. largs saw haggs. tongue saw luss. mull saw yell. stoer
saw strone. drem saw muck. gask saw noss. unst saw cults. echt
saw banff. weem saw wick. trool saw twatt.

how far?
from largo to lunga from joppa to skibo from ratho to shona
from ulva to minto from tinto to tolsta from soutra to marsco
from braco to barra from alva to stobo from fogo to fada from
gigha to gogo from kelso to stroma from hirta to spango.

what is it like there?
och, it's freuchie, it's faifley, it's wamphray, it's frandy, it's
sliddery.

what do you do?
we foindle and fungle, we bonkle and meigle and maxpoffle.
we scotstarvit, armit, wormit, and even whifflet. we play at
crossstobs, leuchars, gorbals, and finfan. we scavaig, and there's
aye a bit of tilquhilly. if it's wet, treshnish and mishnish.

what is the best of the country?
blinkbonny! airgold! thundergay!

and the worst?
scrishven, shiskine, scrabster, and snizort.

listen! what's that?
catacol and wauchope, never heed them.

tell us about last night
well, we had a wee ferintosh and we lay on the quiraing. it was
pure strontian!

but who was there?
petermoidart and craigenkenneth and cambusputtock and
ecclemuchty and corriehulish and balladolly and altnacanny
and clauchanvrechan and stronachlochan and auchenlachar and
tighnacrankie and tilliebruaich and killieharra and invervannach
and achnatudlem and machrishellach and inchtamurchan
and auchterfechan and kinlochculter and ardnawhallie and
invershuggle.

and what was the toast?
schiehallion! schiehallion! schiehallion!

TO JOAN EARDLEY

Pale yellow letters
humbly straggling across
the once brilliant red
of a broken shop-face
CONFECTIO
and a blur of children
at their games, passing,
gazing as they pass
at the blur of sweets
in the dingy, cosy
Rottenrow window –
an Eardley on my wall.
Such rags and streaks
that master us! –
that fix what the pick
and bulldozer have crumbled
to a dingier dust,
the living blur
fiercely guarding
energy that has vanished,
cries filling still
the unechoing close!
I wandered by the rubble
and the houses left standing
kept a chill, dying life
in their islands of stone.
No window opened
as the coal cart rolled
and the coalman's call
fell coldly to the ground.
But the shrill children
jump on my wall.

LINOLEUM CHOCOLATE

Two girls running,
running laughing,
laughing lugging
two rolls of linoleum
along London Road –
a bar of chocolate
flies from the pocket
of the second, and a man
picks it up for her, she takes it
and is about to pocket it
but then unwraps it
and the girls have a bite
to recruit the strength
of their giggling progress.

GOOD FRIDAY

Three o'clock. The bus lurches
round into the sun. 'D's this go –'
he flops beside me – 'right along Bath Street?
– Oh tha's, tha's all right, see I've
got to get some Easter eggs for the kiddies.
I've had a wee drink, ye understand –
ye'll maybe think it's a – funny day
to be celebrating – well, no, but ye see
I wasny working, and I like to celebrate
when I'm no working – I don't say it's right
I'm no saying it's right, ye understand – ye understand?
But anyway tha's the way I look at it –
I'm no boring you, eh? – ye see today,
take today, I don't know what today's in aid of,
whether Christ was – crucified or was he –
rose fae the dead like, see what I mean?
You're an educatit man, you can tell me –
– Aye, well. There ye are. It's been seen
time and again, the working man
has nae education, he jist canny – jist
hasny got it, know what I mean,
he's jist bliddy ignorant – Christ aye,
bliddy ignorant. Well –'The bus brakes violently,
he lunges for the stair, swings down – off,
into the sun for his Easter eggs,
on very
          nearly
                    steady
                              legs.

THE STARLINGS IN GEORGE SQUARE

I

Sundown on the high stonefields!
The darkening roofscape stirs –
thick – alive with starlings
gathered singing in the square –
like a shower of arrows they cross
the flash of a western window,
they bead the wires with jet,
they nestle preening by the lamps
and shine, sidling by the lamps
and sing, shining, they stir
the homeward hurrying crowds.
A man looks up and points
smiling to his son beside him
wide-eyed at the clamour on those cliffs –
it sinks, shrills out in waves,
levels to a happy murmur,
scatters in swooping arcs,
a stab of confused sweetness
that pierces the boy like a story,
a story more than a song.
He will never forget that evening,
the silhouette of the roofs,
the starlings by the lamps.

11

The City Chambers are hopping mad.
Councillors with rubber plugs in their ears!
Secretaries closing windows!
Window-cleaners want protection and danger money.
The Lord Provost can't hear herself think, man.
What's that?
Lord Provost, can't hear herself think.

At the General Post Office
the clerks write Three Pounds Starling in the savings-books.
Each telephone-booth is like an aviary.
I tried to send a parcel to County Kerry but –
The cables to Cairo got fankled, sir.
What's that?
I said the cables to Cairo got fankled.

And as for the City Information Bureau –
I'm sorry I can't quite chirrup did you twit –
No I wanted to twee but perhaps you can't cheep –
Would you try once again, that's better, I – sweet –
When's the last boat to Milngavie? Tweet?
What's that?
I said when's the last boat to Milngavie?

III

There is nothing for it now but scaffolding:
clamp it together, send for the bird-men,
Scarecrow Strip for the window-ledge landings,
Cameron's Repellent on the overhead wires.
Armour our pediments against eavesdroppers.
This is a human outpost. Save our statues.
Send back the jungle. And think of the joke:
as it says in the papers, It is very comical
to watch them alight on the plastic rollers
and take a tumble. So it doesn't kill them?
All right, so who's complaining? This isn't Peking
where they shoot the sparrows for hygiene and cash.
So we're all humanitarians, locked in our cliff-dwellings
encased in our repellent, guano-free and guilt-free.
The Lord Provost sings in her marble hacienda.
The Postmaster-General licks an audible stamp.
Sir Walter is vexed that his column's deserted.
I wonder if we really deserve starlings?
There is something to be said for these joyous messengers
that we repel in our indignant orderliness.
They lift up the eyes, they lighten the heart,
and some day we'll decipher that sweet frenzied whistling
as they wheel and settle along our hard roofs
and take those grey buttresses for home.
One thing we know they say, after their fashion.
They like the warm cliffs of man.

KING BILLY

Grey over Riddrie the clouds piled up,
dragged their rain through the cemetery trees.
The gates shone cold. Wind rose
flaring the hissing leaves, the branches
swung, heavy, across the lamps.
Gravestones huddled in drizzling shadow,
flickering streetlight scanned the requiescats,
a name and an urn, a date, a dove
picked out, lost, half-regained.
What is this dripping wreath, blown from its grave
red, white, blue, and gold
'To Our Leader of Thirty Years Ago' –

Bareheaded, in dark suits, with flutes
and drums, they brought him here, in procession
seriously, King Billy of Brigton, dead,
from Bridgeton Cross: a memory of violence,
brooding days of empty bellies,
billiard smoke and a sour pint,
boots or fists, famous sherrickings,
the word, the scuffle, the flash, the shout,
bloody crumpling in the close,
bricks for papish windows, get
the Conks next time, the Conks ambush
the Billy Boys, the Billy Boys the Conks till
Sillitoe scuffs the razors down the stank –
No, but it isn't the violence they remember
but the legend of a violent man
born poor, gang-leader in the bad times
of idleness and boredom, lost in better days,
a bouncer in a betting club,
a quiet man at last, dying
alone in Bridgeton in a box bed.

So a thousand people stopped the traffic
for the hearse of a folk hero and the flutes
threw 'Onward Christian Soldiers' to the winds
from unironic lips, the mourners kept
in step, and there were some who wept.

Go from the grave. The shrill flutes
Are silent, the march dispersed.
Deplore what is to be deplored,
and then find out the rest.

GLASGOW GREEN

Clammy midnight, moonless mist.
A cigarette glows and fades on a cough.
Meth-men mutter on benches,
pawed by river fog. Monteith Row
sweats coldly, crumbles, dies
slowly. All shadows are alive.
Somewhere a shout's forced out – 'No!' –
it leads to nothing but silence,
except the whisper of the grass
and the other whispers that fill the shadows.

'What d'ye mean see me again?
D'ye think I came here jist for that?
I'm no finished with you yet.
I can get the boys t'ye, they're no that faur away.
You wouldny like that eh? Look there's no two ways aboot it.
Christ but I'm gaun to have you Mac
if it takes all night, turn over you bastard
turn over, I'll –'

Cut the scene.
Here there's no crying for help,
it must be acted out, again, again.

This is not the delicate nightmare
you carry to the point of fear
and wake from, it is life, the sweat
is real, the wrestling under a bush
is real, the dirty starless river
is the real Clyde, with a dishrag dawn
it rinses the horrors of the night
but cannot make them clean,
though washing blows
                              where the women watch
by day,
        and children run,
                              on Glasgow Green.

And how shall these men live?
Providence, watch them go!
Watch them love, and watch them die!
How shall the race be served?
It shall be served by anguish
as well as by children at play.
It shall be served by loneliness
as well as by family love.
It shall be served by hunter and hunted in their endless chain
as well as by those who turn back the sheets in peace.
The thorn in the flesh!
Providence, water it!
Do you think it is not watered?
Do you think it is not planted?
Do you think there is not a seed of the thorn
as there is also a harvest of the thorn?

Man, take in that harvest!
Help that tree to bear its fruit!
Water the wilderness, walk there, reclaim it!
Reclaim, regain, renew! Fill the barns and the vats!

Longing,
            longing
                        shall find its wine.

Let the women sit in the Green
and rock their prams as the sheets
blow and whip in the sunlight.
But the beds of married love
are islands in a sea of desire.
Its waves break here, in this park,
splashing the flesh as it trembles
like driftwood through the dark.

IN THE SNACK-BAR

A cup capsizes along the formica,
slithering with a dull clatter.
A few heads turn in the crowded evening snack-bar.
An old man is trying to get to his feet
from the low round stool fixed to the floor.
Slowly he levers himself up, his hands have no power.
He is up as far as he can get. The dismal hump
looming over him forces his head down.
He stands in his stained beltless gaberdine
like a monstrous animal caught in a tent
in some story. He sways slightly,
the face not seen, bent down

in shadow under his cap.
Even on his feet he is staring at the floor
or would be, if he could see.
I notice now his stick, once painted white
but scuffed and muddy, hanging from his right arm.
Long blind, hunchback born, half paralysed
he stands
fumbling with the stick
and speaks:
'I want – to go to the – toilet.'

It is down two flights of stairs, but we go.
I take his arm. 'Give me – your arm – it's better,' he says.
Inch by inch we drift towards the stairs.
A few yards of floor are like a landscape
to be negotiated, in the slow setting out
time has almost stopped. I concentrate
my life to his: crunch of spilt sugar,
slidy puddle from the night's umbrellas,
table edges, people's feet,
hiss of the coffee-machine, voices and laughter,
smell of a cigar, hamburgers, wet coats steaming,
and the slow dangerous inches to the stairs.
I put his right hand on the rail
and take his stick. He clings to me. The stick
is in his left hand, probing the treads.
I guide his arm and tell him the steps.
And slowly we go down. And slowly we go down.
White tiles and mirrors at last. He shambles
uncouth into the clinical gleam.
I set him in position, stand behind him
and wait with his stick.
His brooding reflection darkens the mirror
but the trickle of his water is thin and slow,

an old man's apology for living.
Painful ages to close his trousers and coat –
I do up the last buttons for him.
He asks doubtfully, 'Can I – wash my hands?'
I fill the basin, clasp his soft fingers round the soap.
He washes, feebly, patiently. There is no towel.
I press the pedal of the drier, draw his hands
gently into the roar of the hot air.
But he cannot rub them together,
drags out a handkerchief to finish.
He is glad to leave the contraption, and face the stairs.
He climbs, and steadily enough.
He climbs, we climb. He climbs
with many pauses but with that one
persisting patience of the undefeated
which is the nature of man when all is said.
And slowly we go up. And slowly we go up.
The faltering, unfaltering steps
take him at last to the door
across that endless, yet not endless waste of floor.
I watch him helped on a bus. He shudders off in the rain.
The conductor bends to hear where he wants to go.

Wherever he could go it would be dark
and yet he must trust men.
Without embarrassment or shame
he must announce his most pitiful needs
in a public place. No one sees his face.
Does he know how frightening he is in his strangeness
under his mountainous coat, his hands like wet leaves
stuck to the half-white stick?
His life depends on many who would evade him.
But he cannot reckon up the chances,
having one thing to do,

to haul his blind hump through these rains of August.
Dear Christ, to be born for this!

TRIO

Coming up Buchanan Street, quickly, on a sharp winter evening
a young man and two girls, under the Christmas lights –
The young man carries a new guitar in his arms,
the girl on the inside carries a very young baby,
and the girl on the outside carries a chihuahua.
And the three of them are laughing, their breath rises
in a cloud of happiness, and as they pass
the boy says, 'Wait till he sees this but!'
The chihuahua has a tiny Royal Stewart tartan coat like a teapot-holder,
the baby in its white shawl is all bright eyes and mouth like favours in a
        fresh sweet cake,
the guitar swells out under its milky plastic cover, tied at the neck
        with silver tinsel tape and a brisk sprig of mistletoe.
Orphean sprig! Melting baby! Warm chihuahua!
The vale of tears is powerless before you.
Whether Christ is born, or is not born, you
put paid to fate, it abdicates
                              under the Christmas lights.
Monsters of the year
go blank, are scattered back,
can't bear this march of three.

– And the three have passed, vanished in the crowd
(yet not vanished, for in their arms they wind
the life of men and beasts, and music,
laughter ringing them round like a guard)
at the end of this winter's day.

But does every man feel like this at forty –
I mean it's like Thomas Wolfe's New York, his
heady light, the stunning plunging canyons, beauty –
pale stars winking hazy downtown quitting-time,
and the winter moon flooding the skyscrapers, northern –
an aspiring place, glory of the bridges, foghorns
are enormous messages, a looming mastery
that lays its hand on the young man's bowels
until he feels in that air, that rising spirit
all things are possible, he rises with it
until he feels that he can never die –
Can it be like this, and is this what it means
in Glasgow now, writing as the aircraft roar
over building sites, in this warm west light
by the daffodil banks that were never so crowded and lavish –
green May, and the slow great blocks rising
under yellow tower cranes, concrete and glass and steel
out of a dour rubble it was and barefoot children gone –
Is it only the slow stirring, a city's renewed life
that stirs me, could it stir me so deeply
as May, but could May have stirred
what I feel of desire and strength
like an arm saluting a sun?

All January, all February the skaters
enjoyed Bingham's pond, the crisp cold evenings,
they swung and flashed among car headlights,
the drivers parked round the unlit pond
to watch them, and give them light, what laughter
and pleasure rose in the rare lulls
of the yards-away stream of wheels along Great Western Road!
The ice broke up, but the boats came out.
The painted boats are ready for pleasure.

The long light needs no headlamps.

Black oar cuts a glitter: it is heaven on earth.

Is it true that we come alive
not once, but many times?
We are drawn back to the image
of the seed in darkness, or the greying skin
of the snake that hides a shining one –
it will push that used-up matter off
and even the film of the eye is sloughed –
That the world may be the same, and we are not
and so the world is not the same,
the second eye is making again
this place, these waters and these towers,
they are rising again
as the eye stands up to the sun,
as the eye salutes the sun.

Many things are unspoken
in the life of a man, and with a place
there is an unspoken love also
in undercurrents, drifting, waiting its time.
A great place and its people are not renewed lightly.
The caked layers of grime
grow warm, like homely coats.
But yet they will be dislodged
and men will still be warm.
The old coats are discarded.
The old ice is loosed.
The old seeds are awake.

Slip out of darkness, it is time.

THE UNSPOKEN

When the troopship was pitching round the Cape
in '41, and there was a lull in the night uproar of seas and winds,
    and a sudden full moon
swung huge out of the darkness like the world it is,
and we all crowded onto the wet deck, leaning on the rail, our arms
    on each other's shoulders, gazing at the savage outcrop of great Africa,
and Tommy Cosh started singing 'Mandalay' and we joined in
    with our raucous chorus of the unforgettable song,
and the dawn came up like thunder like that moon drawing the water of our
    yearning
though we were going to war, and left us exalted,
that was happiness,
but it is not like that.

When the television newscaster said
the second sputnik was up, not empty
but with a small dog on board,
a half-ton treasury of life orbiting a thousand miles above the thin
    television masts and mists of November,
in clear space, heard, observed,
the faint far heartbeat sending back its message
steady and delicate,
and I was stirred by a deep confusion of feelings,
got up, stood with my back to the wall and my palms pressed hard
    against it, my arms held wide
as if I could spring from this earth –
not loath myself to go out that very day where Laika had shown man,
felt my cheeks burning with old Promethean warmth
rekindled – ready –
covered my face with my hands, seeing only an animal
strapped in a doomed capsule, but the future
was still there, cool and whole like the moon,

waiting to be taken, smiling even
as the dog's bones and the elaborate casket of aluminium
glow white and fuse in the arc of re-entry,
and I knew what I felt was history,
its thrilling brilliance came down,
came down,
comes down on us all, bringing pride and pity,
but it is not like that.

But Glasgow days and grey weathers, when the rain
beat on the bus shelter and you leaned slightly against me, and the
    back of your hand touched my hand in the shadows, and
    nothing was said,
when your hair grazed mine accidentally as we talked in a café,
    yet not quite accidentally,
when I stole a glance at your face as we stood in a doorway and found I was afraid
of what might happen if I should never see it again,
when we met, and met, in spite of such differences in our lives,
and did the common things that in our feeling
became extraordinary, so that our first kiss
was like the winter morning moon, and as you shifted in my arms
it was the sea changing the shingle that changes it
as if for ever (but we are bound by nothing, but like smoke
to mist or light in water we move, and mix) –
O then it was a story as old as war or man,
and although we have not said it we know it,
and although we have not claimed it we do it,
and although we have not vowed it we keep it,
without a name to the end.

FROM A CITY BALCONY

How often when I think of you the day grows bright!
Our silent love
wanders in Glen Fruin with the butterflies and cuckoos –
bring me the drowsy country thing! Let it drift above the traffic
by the open window with a cloud of witnesses –
a sparkling burn, white lambs, the blaze of gorse,
the cuckoos calling madly, the real white clouds over us,
white butterflies about your hand in the short hot grass,
and then the witness was my hand closing on yours,
my mouth brushing your eyelids and your lips
again and again till you sighed and turned for love.
Your breast and thighs were blazing like the gorse.
I covered your great fire in silence there.
We let the day grow old along the grass.
It was in the silence the love was.

Footsteps and witnesses! In this Glasgow balcony who pours
such joy like mountain water? It brims, it spills over and over
down to the parched earth and the relentless wheels.
How often will I think of you, until
our dying steps forget this light, forget
that we ever knew the happy glen,
or that I ever said, We must jump into the sun,
and we jumped into the sun.

WHEN YOU GO

When you go,
if you go,
and I should want to die,
there's nothing I'd be saved by
more than the time
you fell asleep in my arms
in a trust so gentle
I let the darkening room
drink up the evening, till
rest, or the new rain
lightly roused you awake.
I asked if you heard the rain in your dream
and half dreaming still you only said, I love you.

STRAWBERRIES

There were never strawberries
like the ones we had
that sultry afternoon
sitting on the step
of the open french window
facing each other
your knees held in mine
the blue plates in our laps
the strawberries glistening
in the hot sunlight
we dipped them in sugar
looking at each other
not hurrying the feast
for one to come
the empty plates

laid on the stone together
with the two forks crossed
and I bent towards you
sweet in that air
in my arms
abandoned like a child
from your eager mouth
the taste of strawberries
in my memory
lean back again
let me love you

let the sun beat
on our forgetfulness
one hour of all
the heat intense
and summer lightning
on the Kilpatrick hills

let the storm wash the plates

ONE CIGARETTE

No smoke without you, my fire.
After you left,
your cigarette glowed on in my ashtray
and sent up a long thread of such quiet grey
I smiled to wonder who would believe its signal
of so much love. One cigarette
in the non-smoker's tray.
As the last spire
trembles up, a sudden draught

blows it winding into my face.
Is it smell, is it taste?
You are here again, and I am drunk on your tobacco lips.
Out with the light.
Let the smoke lie back in the dark.
Till I hear the very ash
sigh down among the flowers of brass
I'll breathe, and long past midnight, your last kiss.

IN SOBIESKI'S SHIELD

well the prophets were dancing in the end much
good it did them and the sun didn't rise at all
anywhere but we weren't among the frozen we had been
dematerialized the day before solar withdrawal
in a hurry it's true but by the best technique
who said only technique well anyhow the best
available and here we are now rematerialized
to the best of my knowledge on a minor planet
of a sun in Sobieski's Shield in our right mind I hope
approximately though not unshaken and admittedly
not precisely those who set out if one can
speak of it by that wellworn tellurian euphemism
in any case molecular reconstitution is no
sinecure even with mice and I wouldn't have been
utterly surprised if some of us had turned out
mice or worse

but at least not that or not yet the effects
of violent change are still slightly present an
indescribable stringent sensation like perhaps being
born or dying but no neither of these I am

very nearly who I was I see I have only
four fingers on my left hand and there's a sharp
twinge I never had in my knee and one most curious
I almost said birthmark and so it is in a sense
light brown shaped like a crazy heart spreading
across my right forearm well let it be we are
here my wife my son the rest of the laboratory
my wife has those streaks of fiery red in her
hair that is expected in women she looks very
frightened yet and lies rigid the rematerialization
is slow in her but that is probably better yes
her eyes flutter to mine questioning I nod can I
smile I think I can does she see me yes thank god
she is hardly altered apart from that extraordinarily
strange and beautiful crown of bright red hair
I draw her head into my arms and hide the sobbing
shuddering first breaths of her second life I don't
know what made me use that phrase who are we
if we are not who we were we have only
one life though we are huddled now in our
protective dome on this harsh metallic plain
that belches cobalt from its craters under a
white-bronze pulsing gong of a sun it was all
they could do for us light-years away it seemed suitable
dematerialization's impossible over short distances anyway
so let's start moving I can surely get onto my feet
yes hoy there

my son is staring fascinated at my four fingers
you've only one nipple I tell him and it's true
but for compensation when he speaks his boy's
treble has broken and at thirteen he is a man
what a limbo to lose childhood in where has
it gone between the throwing of a switch and these

alien iron hills across so many stars his blue eyes
are the same but there's a new graveness of the
second life that phrase again we go up together
to the concave of the dome the environment after all
has to be studied

is that a lake of mercury I can't quite see
through the smoke of the fumarole it's lifting now
but there's something puzzling even when I
my memory of mercury seems to be confused with
what is it blood no no mercury's not like blood
what then what is it I'm remembering or nearly
remembering look dad mercury he says and so it
must be but I see a shell-hole filled with rain-water
red in the sinking sun I know that landscape too
one of the wars far back twentieth century I think the
great war was it called France Flanders fields I remember
reading these craters waterlogged with rain mud blood
I can see a stark hand brandishing nothing through placid scum
in a lull of the guns what horror that the livid water
is not shaken by the pity of the tattoo on the dead arm
a heart still held above the despair of the mud
my god the heart on my arm my second birth mark
the rematerialization has picked up these fragments I have
a graft of war and ancient agony forgive
me my dead helper

the sulky pool of mercury stares back at me I am
seeing normally now but I know these flashes will return
from the far past times I gather my wife and son to me
with a fierce gesture that surprises them I am not
a demonstrative man yet how to tell them
what and who I am that we are bound to all that lived
though the barriers are unspeakable we know a little of that

but something what is it gets through it is not
an essence but an energy how it pierces how it
clutches for still as I run my hand through her
amazing hair streaming on my shoulder I feel
a fist shaken in a shell-hole turn in my very marrow
we shall live in the rings of this chain the jeremiahs
who said nothing human would stand are confounded if I cry
even the dry tear in my heart that I cannot
stop or if I laugh to think they thought they
could divide the indivisible the old moon's in
the new moon's arms let's take our second
like our first life out from the dome are the suits
ready the mineral storm is quieter it's hard
to go let's go

FROM THE DOMAIN OF ARNHEIM

And so that all these ages, these years
we cast behind us, like the smoke-clouds
dragged back into vacancy when the rocket springs –

The domain of Arnheim was all snow, but we were there.
We saw a yellow light thrown on the icefield
from the huts by the pines, and laughter came up
floating from a white corrie
miles away, clearly.
We moved on down, arm in arm,
I know you would have thought it was a dream
but we were there. And those were trumpets –
tremendous round the rocks –
while they were burning fires of trash and mammoths' bones.
They sang naked, and kissed in the smoke.

A child, or one of their animals, was crying.
Young men blew the ice crystals off their drums.
We came down among them, but of course
they could see nothing, on their time-scale.
Yet they sensed us, stopped, looked up – even into our eyes.
To them we were a displacement of the air,
a sudden chill, yet we had no power
over their fear. If one of them had been dying
he would have died. The crying
came from one just born: that was the cause
of the song. We saw it now. What had we stopped
but joy?
I know you felt
the same dismay, you gripped my arm, they were waiting
for what they knew of us to pass.
A sweating trumpeter took
a brand from the fire with a shout and threw it
where our bodies would have been –
we felt nothing but his courage.
And so they would deal with every imagined power
seen or unseen.
There are no gods in the domain of Arnheim.

We signalled to the ship; got back;
our lives and days returned to us, but
haunted by deeper souvenirs than any rocks or seeds.
From time the souvenirs are deeds.

what I love about dormice is their size
what I hate about rain is its sneer
what I love about the Bratach Gorm is its unflappability
what I hate about scent is its smell
what I love about newspapers is their etaoin shrdl
what I hate about philosophy is its pursed lip
what I love about Rory is his old grouse
what I hate about Pam is her pinkie
what I love about semi-precious stones is their preciousness
what I hate about diamonds is their mink
what I love about poetry is its ion engine
what I hate about hogs is their setae
what I love about love is its porridge-spoon
what I hate about hate is its eyes
what I love about hate is its salts
what I hate about love is its dog
what I love about Hank is his string vest
what I hate about the twins is their three gloves
what I love about Mabel is her teeter
what I hate about gooseberries is their look, feel, smell, and taste
what I love about the world is its shape
what I hate about a gun is its lock, stock, and barrel
what I love about bacon-and-eggs is its predictability
what I hate about derelict buildings is their reluctance to disintegrate
what I love about a cloud is its unpredictability
what I hate about you, chum, is your china
what I love about many waters is their inability to quench love

GLASGOW 5 MARCH 1971

With a ragged diamond
of shattered plate-glass
a young man and his girl
are falling backwards into a shop-window.
The young man's face
is bristling with fragments of glass
and the girl's leg has caught
on the broken window
and spurts arterial blood
over her wet-look white coat.
Their arms are starfished out
braced for impact,
their faces show surprise, shock,
and the beginning of pain.
The two youths who have pushed them
are about to complete the operation
reaching into the window
to loot what they can smartly.
Their faces show no expression.
It is a sharp clear night
in Sauchiehall Street.
In the background two drivers
keep their eyes on the road.

VENICE APRIL 1971

Three black gondolas
cut the sparkle of the lagoon.

In the first, the Greek archimandrite
stands, a young black-bearded man
in gold cope, black hood, black shoulder veil blown back
in the sunny breeze. In front of him
his even younger acolyte holds high
the glittering processional cross. His long black robe
glitters with delicious silver flowers
against the blue of the sky.

In the second gondola Stravinsky goes.
The black fringe trails the lapping water,
the heavy coffin dips the golden lions on the sides,
the gondoliers are ankle-deep in roses,
the coffin sways crowned with roses,
the gondoliers' white blouses and black sashes
startle their brown arms, the shining oars,
the pink and crimson flowers.

And the third gondola
is like a shadow
where the widow goes.

And there at the edge of the picture
where the crowds cross themselves
and weep a little in the Italian way,
an old poet with white hair
and hooded, piercing eyes
leans on his stick
and without expression
watches the boats move out
from his shore.

At the Festival of Islam
the dervishes are dancing.
The dancemaster stands
in his long black gown
straight-backed, his hands
folded in front of him.
Twelve swarthy men
in cylindrical hats
and loose white blouses
and long white skirts
and their long white sleeves
stretched out straight
like the albatross
have begun to dance.
The drum measures
flutes and strings
and men following.
Serious, rapt,
as if to wind themselves
up with their arms
they revolve, their skirts
flaring out loose
in white pyramids
below the inverted
pyramids of white
blouses and arms
which support the top
truncated pyramids
of circling hats.

Pattern and no pattern,
alone and in union
without unison
in the hard light
of Friends' House
in Euston Road
the dervishes whirl
round, they dance
round, round
they go, without
sound, now,
round and round.

DONA EMA BRAZIL APRIL 1972

In a cabin of sweet cedarwood
deep in an orange-grove
an old Hungarian doctor-poet, dying,
is writing his last quirky postcard
to an English friend. His brown eyes twinkle
as he thinks of his thirteen languages,
his theory of pain, his use of hypnosis
in childbirth, his work with the Resistance
in Italy, his wryest fame in *Winnie*
Ille Pu, his end
in a nest of lianas.
With a laugh he stops
just short of the date
which who cares who will add.
ALEXANDER LENARD, says the card,
obiit, meghalt, starb, mori, died.

DARMSTADT SEPTEMBER 1972

A middle-aged precision instrument mechanic
having fallen behind with the mortgage repayments
on a fine new house, has kitted up
the workbench in his study
with a home-made, but well-made
guillotine, the blade
a nicely slicing two-feet-long steel
paper-trimmer, the weight
a tested squat steel
anvil, the complex of ropes
designed to release the trimmer
with a perfectly shimmering swish of
descent on the neck as he lies
prone on the bench, and
like a precision instrument
he has pulled the rope
so delicately that his head,
though severed, sits still
on the board. It looks straight
at his wife standing in the door.

GLASGOW OCTOBER 1972

At the Old Ship Bank pub in Saltmarket
a milk-lapping contest is in progress.
A dozen very assorted Bridgeton cats
have sprung from their starting-blocks
to get their heads down in the gleaming saucers.
In the middle of the picture
young Tiny is about to win his bottle of whisky
by kittening through the sweet half-gill
in one minute forty seconds flat, but
Sarah, at the end of the line,
self-contained and silver-grey,
has sat down with her back to the saucer
and surveys the photographers calmly.
She is a cat who does not like milk.

ANDES MOUNTAINS DECEMBER 1972

FUERZA AEREA URUG –
nothing more can be read on the fuselage,
tailless, wingless, a jagged cylinder
at rest in a wilderness of snow and rock.
A rugby charter from Montevideo,
the Old Christians and their supporters.
Two months after the crash, it would not seem
a bleak scene
as the sixteen tough surviving young Old Christians
crouch in the mouth of the cylinder,
sipping cups of melted snow and cherry wine,
eating quickly from plastic air force plates,
but for the yellow hands
and feet all round them

48

in the snow, and skulls. The plane's
fire-axe stands in today's body. The shell
where the sweet brain had been is scooped clean.
Razors have flayed the limbs in strips.
A dozen of the dead
have played their part, a dozen more
are laid out, snow-packed, in neat rows
like fish in a box. Cherry wine and blood
are as one on their chins as the flesh
they bless becomes Old Christians.

COLUMBA'S SONG

Where's Brude? Where's Brude?
So many souls to be saved!
The bracken is thick, the wildcat is quick,
the foxes dance in the moonlight,
the salmon dance in the waters,
the adders dance in the thick brown bracken.
Where's Brude? Where's man?
There's too much nature here,
eagles and deer,
but where's the mind and where's the soul?
Show me your kings, your women, the man of the plough.
And cry me to your cradles.
It wasn't for a fox or an eagle I set sail!

If only we'd been strangers
we'd be floating off to Timor,
we'd be shimmering on the Trades
in a blue jersey boat
with shandies, flying fish,
a pace of dolphins
to the copra ports.
And it's no use crying
to me, What dolphins?
I know where they are
and I'd have snapped you up
and carried you away
snapped you up
and carried you away
if we had been strangers.

But here we are care
of the black roofs.
It's not hard to find
with a collar turned up
and a hoot from the Clyde.
The steps come home
whistling too. And a kettle
steams the cranes out slowly.
It's living with ships
makes a rough springtime
and who is safe
when they sing and blow
their music – they seem
to swing at some light rope
like those desires
we keep for strangers.
God, the yellow deck

breathes, it heaves spray
back like a shout.
We're cutting through
some straits of the world
in our old dark room
with salty wings
in the shriek of the dock wind.
But we're caught – meshed
in the fish-scales, ferries,
mudflats, lifebelts
fading into football cries
and the lamps coming on
to bring us in.

We take in
the dream, a cloth from the line
the trains fling sparks on
in our city. We're better awake.
But you know I'd take
you all the same,
if you were my next stranger.

IN GLASGOW

In my smoochy corner
take me on a cloud
I'll wrap you round
and lay you down
in smoky tinfoil
rings and records
sheets of whisky
and the moon all right
old pal all right
the moon all night

Mercy for the rainy
tyres and the violet
thunder that bring you
shambling and shy
from chains of Easterhouse
plains of lights
make your delight
in my nest my spell
my arms and my shell
my barn my bell

I've combed your hair
and washed your feet
and made you turn
like a dark eel
in my white bed
till morning lights
a silent cigarette
throw on your shirt
I lie staring yet
forget forget

OBAN GIRL

A girl in a window eating a melon
eating a melon and painting a picture
painting a picture and humming Hey Jude
humming Hey Jude as the light was fading

In the autumn she'll be married

THE APPLE'S SONG

Tap me with your finger,
rub me with your sleeve,
hold me, sniff me, peel me
curling round and round
till I burst out white and cold
from my tight red coat
and tingle in your palm
as if I'd melt and breathe
a living pomander
waiting for the minute
of joy when you lift me
to your mouth and crush me
and in taste and fragrance
I race through your head
in my dizzy dissolve.

I sit in the bowl
in my cool corner
and watch you as you pass
smoothing your apron.
Are you thirsty yet?
My eyes are shining.

DRIFT

Rhododendron dust rose
and fell in the June wind –
lightness, lightness!
And with an arm I
swept the loch away
from your eyes. Drowsy
picnic-fires, the cars,
the wood-pigeon, the spray
of water-skiers through the trees
went fading tangled
off the world.
Only stars of heat
pricked, and your cigarette
smouldered in the grass
forgotten, its blue pungence
not to be forgotten
blown across our faces
with the rhododendron-drift.
Love, pillow me
by the eastern tree.

AT THE TELEVISION SET

Take care if you kiss me,
you know it doesn't die.
The lamplight reaches out, draws it
blandly – all of it – into fixity,
troops of blue shadows like the soundless gunfight,
yellow shadows like your cheek by the lamp
where you lie watching, half watching
between the yellow and the blue.
I half see you, half know you.
Take care if you turn now to face me.
For even in this room we are moving out through stars
and forms that never let us back, your hand
lying lightly on my thigh and my hand on your shoulder
are transfixed only there, not here.

What can you bear that would last
like a rock through cancer and white hair?

Yet it is not easy
to take stock of miseries
when the soft light flickers
along our arms in the stillness
where decisions are made.
You have to look at me,
and then it's time that falls
talking slowly to sleep.

FOR BONFIRES

I

The leaves are gathered, the trees are dying
for a time.
A seagull cries through white smoke in the garden fires
that fill the heavy air.
All day heavy air
is burning, a moody dog
sniffs and circles the swish of the rake.
In streaks of ash, the gardener drifting
ghostly, beats his hands, a cloud
of breath to the red sun.

I I

An island in the city, happy demolition men
behind windowed hoardings – look at them
trailing drills through rubble dust, kicking rubble,
smoking leaning on a pick, putting the stub
over an ear and the hot yellow helmet over that,
whistling up the collapsing chimney, kicking the
ricochet, rattling the trail with
snakes of wire, slamming slabs
down, plaster, cornice, brick, brick
on broken brick and plaster dust,
sprawling with steaming cans and pieces
at noon, afternoon bare sweat shining
paths down chalky backs, coughing
in filtered sunshine, slithering, swearing,
joking, slowly stacking and building
their rubbish into a total bonfire.
Look at that Irishman, bending

in a beautiful arc to throw
the last black rafter to the top,
stands back, walks round it singing
as it crackles into flame – old doors,
old beams, boxes, window-frames,
a rag doll, sacks, flex, old newspapers,
burst shelves, a shoe, old dusters, rags of
wallpaper roses. And they all stand round,
and cheer the tenement to smoke.

III

In a galvanized bucket
the letters burn. They roar and twist
and the leaves curl back one by one.
They put out claws and scrape the iron
like a living thing,
but the scrabbling to be free soon subsides.
The black pages fuse
to a single whispering mass
threaded by dying tracks of gold.
Let them grow cold,
and when they're dead,
quickly draw breath.

BLUE TOBOGGANS

scarves for the apaches
wet gloves for snowballs
whoops for white clouds
and blue toboggans

stamping for a tingle
lamps for four o'clock
steamed glass for buses
and blue toboggans

tuning-forks for Wenceslas
white fogs for Prestwick
mince pies for the Eventides
and blue toboggans

TV for the lonely
a long haul for heaven
a shilling for the gas
and blue toboggans

HYENA

I am waiting for you.
I have been travelling all morning through the bush
and not eaten.
I am lying at the edge of the bush
on a dusty path that leads from the burnt-out kraal.
I am panting, it is midday, I found no water-hole.
I am very fierce without food and although my eyes
are screwed to slits against the sun
you must believe I am prepared to spring.

What do you think of me?
I have a rough coat like Africa.
I am crafty with dark spots
like the bush-tufted plains of Africa.
I sprawl as a shaggy bundle of gathered energy
like Africa sprawling in its waters.
I trot, I lope, I slaver, I am a ranger.
I hunch my shoulders. I eat the dead.

Do you like my song?
When the moon pours hard and cold on the veldt
I sing, and I am the slave of darkness.
Over the stone walls and the mud walls and the ruined places
and the owls, the moonlight falls.
I sniff a broken drum. I bristle. My pelt is silver.
I howl my song to the moon – up it goes.
Would you meet me there in the waste places?

It is said I am a good match
for a dead lion. I put my muzzle
at his golden flanks, and tear. He
is my golden supper, but my tastes are easy.
I have a crowd of fangs, and I use them.
Oh and my tongue – do you like me
when it comes lolling out over my jaw
very long, and I am laughing?
I am not laughing.
But I am not snarling either, only
panting in the sun, showing you
what I grip
carrion with.

I am waiting
for the foot to slide,
for the heart to seize,
for the leaping sinews to go slack,
for the fight to the death to be fought to the death,
for a glazing eye and the rumour of blood.
I am crouching in my dry shadows
till you are ready for me.
My place is to pick you clean
and leave your bones to the wind.

THE LOCH NESS MONSTER'S SONG

Sssnnnwhufffll?
Hnwhuffl hhnnwfl hnfl hfl?
Gdroblboblhobngbl gbl gl g g g g glbgl.
Drublhaflablhaflubhafgabhaflhafl fl fl –
gm grawwwww grf grawf awfgm graw gm.
Hovoplodok-doplodovok-plovodokot-doplodokosh?
Splgraw fok fok splgrafhatchgabrlgabrl fok splfok!
Zgra kra gka fok!
Grof grawff gahf?
Gombl mbl bl –
blm plm,
blm plm,
blm plm,
blp.

Afterwards the sun shone on seven rice shoots and a black tree.

Afterwards the prostitutes fell on lean times / some took up embroidery / one became a pearl-diver and was drowned.

Afterwards my burned little cousin went through eleven grafting operations / never cried.

Afterwards many saffron robes began to be let out / there was a movement to purify the order.

Afterwards the ancient monuments were restored stone by stone / I thought it was folly when I saw the list of legless girls waiting for prosthetic appliances.

Afterwards there was a report of mass ghosts on the plains, all grey as dust, with grey shovels, burying and burying all through the night to the beat of a drum / but in the morning the earth was hard and unbroken.

Afterwards came six great harvests and a glut of fish, and the rivers rolled and steamed through tunnels of fresh green fruit-trees and lilypads needled by kingfishers / rainbow after rainbow plunged into the lakes of rice.

Afterwards I went out with my sister one still hot day into the forest, and we came to an old temple bombed to a shell, with weeds in its windows, and went in hand in hand through a deep rubble of stone and fragments of half-melted statues and rubbish of metal and flowers and bread, and there in a corner we saw the skeleton of a boy, with shreds of blue cotton clinging to the bones, his fingers still clutching the string of a tiny bamboo box / we bent down as a faint chirping started from the box, and saw that it was his grasshopper, alive yet and scraping the only signal it knew from behind the bars of its cage / you said something and burst out crying / I slid the latch then and set it free.

THOUGHTS OF A MODULE

It is black so. There is that dust.
My ladder in light. What are my men.
One is foot down. That is pack drill.
Black what is visor. A hiss I heard.
The talks go up. Clump now but float.
Is a jump near. A camera paced out.
I phase another man. Another man is second.
Second last feet on. The dust I think.
So some soles cross. Is a flag near.
No move yon flag. Which voice comes down.
White house thanks all. Command module man not.
Is kangaroo hop around. I think moon dance.
Or white bird is. Good oxygen I heard.
Earth monitors must be. Is it too pressing.
Trained man is gay. Fail safe is gay.
The black I see. What instruments are lonely.
Sharp is a shadow. A horizon goes flat.
All rock are samples. Dust taken I think.
Is bright my leg. In what sun yonder.
An end I think. How my men go.
The talks come down. The ladder I shake.
To leave that bright. Space dark I see.
Is my men last. Men are that first.
That moon is here. They have some dust.
Is home they know. Blue earth I think.

I lift I see. It is that command.
My men go back. I leave that here.
It is bright so.

THE FIRST MEN ON MERCURY

– We come in peace from the third planet.
Would you take us to your leader?

– Bawr stretter! Bawr. Bawr. Stretterhawl?

– This is a little plastic model
of the solar system, with working parts.
You are here and we are there and we
are now here with you, is this clear?

– Gawl horrop. Bawr. Abawrhannahanna!

 – Where we come from is blue and white
with brown, you see we call the brown
here 'land', the blue is 'sea', and the white
is 'clouds' over land and sea, we live
on the surface of the brown land,
all round is sea and clouds. We are 'men'.
Men come –

– Glawp men! Gawrbenner menko. Menhawl?

– Men come in peace from the third planet
which we call 'earth'. We are earthmen.
Take us earthmen to your leader.

– Thmen? Thmen? Bawr. Bawrhossop.
Yuleeda tan hanna. Harrabost yuleeda.

– I am the yuleeda. You see my hands,
we carry no benner, we come in peace.
The spaceways are all stretterhawn.

 – Glawn peacemen all horrabhanna tantko!
Tan come at'mstrossop. Glawp yuleeda!

– Atoms are peacegawl in our harraban.
Menbat worrabost from tan hannahanna.

– You men we know bawrhossoptant. Bawr.
We know yuleeda. Go strawg backspetter quick.

– We cantantabawr, tantingko backspetter now!

– Banghapper now! Yes, third planet back.
Yuleeda will go back blue, white, brown
nowhanna! There is no more talk.

– Gawl han fasthapper?

– No. You must go back to your planet.
Go back in peace, take what you have gained
but quickly.

 – Stretterworra gawl, gawl…

– Of course, but nothing is ever the same,
now is it? You'll remember Mercury.

SPACEPOEM 3: OFF COURSE

the golden flood   the weightless seat
the cabin song   the pitch black
the growing beard   the floating crumb
the shining rendezvous   the orbit wisecrack
the hot spacesuit   the smuggled mouth-organ
the imaginary somersault   the visionary sunrise
the turning continents   the space debris
the golden lifeline   the space walk
the crawling deltas   the camera moon
the pitch velvet   the rough sleep
the crackling headphone   the space silence
the turning earth   the lifeline continents
the cabin sunrise   the hot flood
the shining spacesuit   the growing moon
   the crackling somersault   the smuggled orbit
   the rough moon   the visionary rendezvous
   the weightless headphone   the cabin debris
   the floating lifeline   the pitch sleep
   the crawling camera   the turning silence
   the space crumb   the crackling beard
   the orbit mouth-organ   the floating song

i

We went to Oldshoremore.
Is the Oldshoremore road still there?
You mean the old shore road?
I suppose it's more an old road than a shore road.
No more! They shored it up, but it's washed away.
So you could sing the old song –
Yes we sang the old song:
  We'll take the old Oldshoremore shore road no more.

ii

We passed the Muckle Flugga.
Did you see the muckle flag?
All we saw was the muckle fog.
The flag says ULTIMA FLUGGA WHA'S LIKE US.
Couldn't see flag for fug, sorry.
Ultimately –
  Ultimately we made for Muck and flogged the lugger.

iii

Was it bleak at Bowhousebog?
It was black as a hoghouse, boy.
Yes, but bleak?
Look, it was black as a bog and bleak as the Bauhaus!
The Bauhaus wasn't black –
Will you get off my back!
So there were dogs too?
  Dogs, hogs, leaks in the bogs – we never went back.

RIDER

i

a grampus whacked the hydrophone / Loch Fyne left its green bed,
   fled / shrieking to Cowal / it all began
the nutcracker closed round Port Glasgow / it snapped with a burst
   of docks and / capstans downwind like collarstuds
cabbage whites in deadlock / were hanged from geans and rowans /
   wedlock-red
Greenock in steam / hammered albatrosses onto packingcases /
   without forgiveness / zam
by the waters of Glasgow / angels hung pilgrims, primroses, Dante,
   black blankets / over and over / the acid streams
a giant hedgehog lifting the Necropolis / solid silver / to the moon /
   sang of the deluge
long keys of gas unlocked the shaking Campsies at / last, at least /
   four drumlins were heard howling / as far as Fenwick Moor
Calderpark was sucked into a belljar, came out / at Kalgoorlie with
   elephants and northern lights
ravening taxis roasted dogs in basements, basted / chicken wheels
   in demolition oil / slept by the swing / of the wrecker's ball
the Holy Loch turned to granite chips, the ships / died with their
   stiff upper lips reaching to Aviemore
Para Handy sculled through the subway with the Stone of Destiny /
   shot the rapids at Cessnock right into Sunday morning
a coelacanth on stilts was setting fire to Sauchiehall Street when
   Tom Leonard /
sold James B.V. Thomson a horse, black /
in the night and dust / which galloped him away /
deep as the grave / writing

ii

Davidson looked through the telescope at MacDiarmid and said /
   what, is that God
Davidson rode off on a blood-splashed stag / into the sea / horses
   ultimately
Davidson sold / fish to Neptune, fire / to Prometheus, to himself /
   a prisoner's iron bed, the red
sun rose flapping slowly over Nietzsche / bars melted into sand /
   black marias stalled in Calton
the rainbow dropped its pot of lead on Peterhead / the peter keys
   were blown to breadcrumbs, fed
to men forbid / the men bought lead, built jails, went mad, lay
   dead / in iron fields
the jaws of Nero smouldered in a dustbin / cinders tingled / the dead
   rose / tamam
sulphur shoes dancing to Mars / their zircon eyeshades flashed,
   beryllium / toeguards clipped Mercury's boulders
Lucretius was found lying under the flary walls / of a universe in the
   Crab nebula / crying
the dancers brought him water / where he lay he rose, froze / in a
   mandala like a flame / blessing
the darkness of all disbelievers / filaments of the Crab wrapped him
   in hydrogen shroud / remade
he walked by Barrhead and Vauxhall Bridge, by the sea waited /
   with his dark horse in the dangerous night air
for a rider / his testament
delivered to the earth, kicking /
the roots of things

five hundred million hummingbirds sat in the Kelvin Hall / three
   hundred thousand girls took double basses
in a crocodile to Inverkip / six thousand children drew Rothesay
   through twelve thousand kites / two hundred
plumbers with morning cellos galvanized the bedmakers of Fairlie /
   forty babies
threw their teething-rings at a helicopter / trickety-track / till
   Orpheus looked back
and there was nothing but the lonely hills and sky unless the chilling
   wind was something / and the space
of pure white pain where his wife had held his hand from hell / he
   left the place
and came to a broken shack at midday / with carts and horses /
   strong dark ragged boys
played in the smoke / the gypsies gave him soup and bread / for the
   divine brooch / who cares
what is divine, he said / and passed into the valley of the Clyde,
   a cloud / followed
and many campfires in that landscape, dogs whining, cuckoos,
   glasshouses, thundershowers /
David Gray shook the rain from his hair and held his heart, the
   Luggie flashed
in the lightning of the last March storm / he led a sweet brown mare
   into the mist / the apple-boughs
closed over, where the flute
of Orpheus was only wished for /
in the drip of trees

iv

butcher-boys tried to ward off sharks / the waters rose quickly /
   great drowned bankers

floated from bay-windows / two housemaids struggled on
   Grosvenor Terrace with a giant conger

the Broomielaw was awash with slime and torn-out claws and
   anchor-flakes / rust and dust

sifted together where a dredger ploughed up the Gallowgate /
   pushed a dirty wave over Shettleston

spinning shopfronts crashed in silence / glassily, massively /
   porticoes tilting / settled in mud

lampreys fastened on four dead sailors drifting through Finnieston /
   in a Drygate attic

James Macfarlan threw his pen at the stinking wall / the whisky and
   the stinking poverty

ran down like ink / the well of rats was bottomless and Scotch / the
   conman and the conned

fought on / the ballads yellowed, the pubs filled / at Anderston he
   reached his grave in snow / selah

the ruined cities were switched off / there was no flood / his father
   led a pedlar's horse

by Carrick fields, his mother sang / the boy rode on a jogging back /
   far back / in rags /

Dixon's Blazes roared and threw more poets in its molten pools /
   forges on fire

matched the pitiless bread, the head

long hangdog, the lifted elbow /

the true bloody pathos and sublime

Kossuth took a coalblack horse from Debrecen / clattered up
   Candleriggs into the City Hall
three thousand cheers could never drown the groaning fortress-
   bars / a thousand years
heard the wind howl / scimitars, eagles, bugles, edicts, whips,
   crowns, in the pipes / playing / the grave plain in the sun
handcuffed keelies shouted in Albion Street / slogans in red
   fragments broke the cobblestones, Kossuth
drew a mirage on electric air / the hare sat calmly on the
   doorstep / it was Monday over all the world / om
Tom McGrath mixed bread and milk for the young hare / Monk
   and Parker spoke in a corner / the still room
was taken / Dougal Graham stood on his hands, the bell / rang
   between his feet / he rolled
on his hump through the swarming Tontine piazzas, swam / in
   dogs, parcels, puddles, tobacco-quids
ran with a bawbee ballad five feet long / felt fishwives / gutted
   a brace of Glasgow magistrates / lay
with a pig in his arms and cried the city fathers bitches / till
   a long shadow fell on pedlars
and far away the sound of hoofs / increased in moonlight / whole
   cities crouched in saddlebags
churches, dungeons, juntas dangled from reins / like grasses
   picked from the rank fields
and drops of halter sweat
burned men to the bone, but the hare
like mad / played

A huddle on the greasy street –
cars stop, nose past, withdraw –
dull glint on soles of tackety boots,
frayed rough blue trousers, nondescript coat
stretching back, head supported
in strangers' arms, a crowd collecting –
'Whit's wrang?' 'Can ye see'm?'
'An auld fella, he's had it.'
On one side, a young mother in a headscarf
is kneeling to comfort him, her three-year-old son
stands puzzled, touching her coat, her shopping-bag
spills its packages that people look at
as they look at everything. On the other side
a youth, nervous, awkwardly now
at the centre of attention as he shifts his arm
on the old man's shoulders, wondering
what to say to him, glancing up at the crowd.
These were next to him when he fell,
and must support him into death.
He seems not to be in pain,
he is speaking slowly and quietly
but he does not look at any of them,
his eyes are fixed on the sky,
already he is moving out
beyond everything belonging.
As if he still belonged
they hold him very tight.

Only the hungry ambulance
howls for him through the staring squares.

CHRISTMAS EVE

Loneliness of city Christmas Eves –
with real stars up there – clear – and stars
on poles and wires across the street, and streaming
cars all dark with parcels, home
to families and the lighted window trees –

I sat down in the bus beside him – white jeans,
black jerkin, slumped with head nodding
in sleep, face hidden by long black hair, hands
tattooed on the four fingers ADEN 1967
and on the right hand five Christian crosses.
As the bus jerked, his hand fell on my knee,
stayed there, lay heavily and alive
with blue carvings from another world
and seemed to hold me like a claw,
unmoving. It moved. I rubbed my ear
to steal a glance at him, found him
stealing a glance at me. It was not
the jerking of the bus, it was a proposition.
He shook his hair back, and I saw his face
for the first time, unshaven, hardman, a warning
whether in Aden or Glasgow, but our eyes held
while that blue hand burned into my leg.
Half drunk, half sleeping – but half what, half what?
As his hand stirred again, my arm covered it
while the bus jolted around the corner.
'Don't ge' aff tae ah ge' aff.' – But the conductor
was watching, came up and shook him, looked at me.
My ticket was up, I had to leave him sprawled there
with that hand that now seemed so defenceless

lying on the seat I had left. Half down the stair
I looked back. The last thing I saw was Aden
and five blue crosses for five dead friends.

It was only fifteen minutes out of life
but I feel as if I was lifted by a whirlwind
and thrown down on some desert rocks to die
of dangers as always far worse lost than run.

GLASGOW SONNETS

i

A mean wind wanders through the backcourt trash.
Hackles on puddles rise, old mattresses
puff briefly and subside. Play-fortresses
of brick and bric-a-brac spill out some ash.
Four storeys have no windows left to smash,
but in the fifth a chipped sill buttresses
mother and daughter the last mistresses
of that black block condemned to stand, not crash.
Around them the cracks deepen, the rats crawl.
The kettle whimpers on a crazy hob.
Roses of mould grow from ceiling to wall.
The man lies late since he has lost his job,
smokes on one elbow, letting his coughs fall
thinly into an air too poor to rob.

ii

A shilpit dog fucks grimly by the close.
Late shadows lengthen slowly, slogans fade.
The YY PARTICK TOI grins from its shade
like the last strains of some lost *libera nos*
a malo. No deliverer ever rose
from these stone tombs to get the hell they made
unmade. The same weans never make the grade.
The same grey street sends back the ball it throws.
Under the darkness of a twisted pram
a cat's eyes glitter. Glittering stars press
between the silent chimney-cowls and cram
the higher spaces with their SOS.
Don't shine a torch on the ragwoman's dram.
Coats keep the evil cold out less and less.

iii

'See a tenement due for demolition?
I can get ye rooms in it, two, okay?
Seven hundred and nothin legal to pay
for it's no legal, see? That's my proposition,
ye can take it or leave it but. The position
is simple, you want a hoose, I say
for eight hundred pound it's yours.' And they
trailing five bairns, accepted his omission
of the foul crumbling stairwell, windows wired
not glazed, the damp from the canal, the cooker
without pipes, packs of rats that never tired –
any more than the vandals bored with snooker
who stripped the neighbouring houses, howled, and fired
their aerosols – of squeaking 'Filthy lucre!'

iv

Down by the brickworks you get warm at least.
Surely soup-kitchens have gone out? It's not
the Thirties now. Hugh MacDiarmid forgot
in 'Glasgow 1960' that the feast
of reason and the flow of soul has ceased
to matter to the long unfinished plot
of heating frozen hands. We never got
an abstruse song that charmed the raging beast.
So you have nothing to lose but your chains,
dear Seventies. Dalmarnock, Maryhill,
Blackhill and Govan, better sticks and stanes
should break your banes, for poets' words are ill
to hurt ye. On the wrecker's ball the rains
of greeting cities drop and drink their fill.

v

'Let them eat cake' made no bones about it.
But we say let them eat the hope deferred
and that will sicken them. We have preferred
silent slipways to the riveters' wit.
And don't deny it – that's the ugly bit.
Ministers' tears might well have launched a herd
of bucking tankers if they'd been transferred
from Whitehall to the Clyde. And smiles don't fit
either. 'There'll be no bevvying' said Reid
at the work-in. But all the dignity you muster
can only give you back a mouth to feed
and rent to pay if what you lose in bluster
is no more than win patience with 'I need'
while distant blackboards use you as their duster.

vi

The North Sea oil-strike tilts east Scotland up,
and the great sick Clyde shivers in its bed.
But elegists can't hang themselves on fled-
from trees or poison a recycled cup –
If only a less faint, shaky sunup
glimmered through the skeletal shop and shed
and men washed round the piers like gold and spread
golder in soul than Mitsubishi or Krupp –
The images are ageless but the thing
is now. Without my images the men
ration their cigarettes, their children cling
to broken toys, their women wonder when
the doors will bang on laughter and a wing
over the firth be simply joy again.

vii

Environmentalists, ecologists
and conservationists are fine no doubt.
Pedestrianization will come out
fighting, riverside walks march off the lists,
pigeons and starlings be somnambulists
in far-off suburbs, the sandblaster's grout
multiply pink piebald façades to pout
at sticky-fingered mock-Venetianists.
Prop up's the motto. Splint the dying age.
Never displease the watchers from the grave.
Great when fake architecture was the rage,
but greater still to see what you can save.
The gutted double fake meets the adage:
a wig's the thing to beat both beard and shave.

viii

Meanwhile the flyovers breed loops of light
in curves that would have ravished tragic Toshy –
clean and unpompous, nothing wishy-washy.
Vistas swim out from the bulldozer's bite
by day, and banks of earthbound stars at night
begin. In Madame Emé's Sauchie Haugh, she
could never gain in leaves or larks or sploshy
lanes what's lost in a dead boarded site –
the life that overspill is overkill to.
Less is not more, and garden cities are
the flimsiest oxymoron to distil to.
And who wanted to distil? Let bus and car
and hurrying umbrellas keep their skill to
feed ukiyo-e beyond Lochnagar.

ix

It groans and shakes, contracts and grows again.
Its giant broken shoulders shrug off rain.
It digs its pits to a shauchling refrain.
Roadworks and graveyards like their gallus men.
It fattens fires and murders in a pen
and lets them out in flaps and squalls of pain.
It sometimes tears its smoky counterpane
to hoist a bleary fist at nothing, then
at everything, you never know. The west
could still be laid with no one's tears like dust
and barricaded windows be the best
to see from till the shops, the ships, the trust
return like thunder. Give the Clyde the rest.
Man and the sea make cities as they must.

x

From thirtieth floor windows at Red Road
he can see choughs and samphires, dreadful trade –
the schoolboy reading *Lear* has that scene made.
A multi is a sonnet stretched to ode
and some say that's no joke. The gentle load
of souls in clouds, vertiginously stayed
above the windy courts, is probed and weighed.
Each monolith stands patient, ah'd and oh'd.
And stalled lifts generating high-rise blues
can be set loose. But stalled lives never budge.
They linger in the single-ends that use
their spirit to the bone, and when they trudge
from closemouth to laundrette their steady shoes
carry a world that weighs us like a judge.

from THE NEW DIVAN

I

Hafiz, old nightingale, what fires there have been
in the groves, white dust, wretchedness,
how could you ever get your song together?
Someone stands by your tomb, thinks
as a shadow thinks: much, little, any?
You swore you'd be found shrouded in another
grave-cloth of pure smoke from a heart as
burning dead as beating, but the names
of cinders are thick where passions were.
Whole cities could be ash. But
not the song the Sufi says we have
but our dying song, you knew, gives us our beings.

6

What a tottering veil to call an expanse
of desire demure by! I love those masses
of satsumas at your elbow, piled like the times
you praise. Beyond the window there's an engine
hissing past the harvest. A girl
walks her dog in mist. Lattices
tingle as you shriek like lightning
when the parrot shrieks and forcibly
detain the coffee-boy. A trail
of grape-seeds vanishes below
the couch. You crouch
on huge all-fours in the balcony sand
and groan and tap your grin with your pipe.

18

Squalls, viziers, cassettes can be obscure.
You want the lyric line, you want the words
to lay their length against you like – like what?
Are we not living in the utterance?
To say I love you as I love you as
I love you is three roses for the cutting:
a little attar of Shiraz always,
the sheets for things unsaid,
the glass bright red. The days awoke, recurred,
the nights recur, awake. The moon. The earth.

26

To take without anxiety the love
you think fate might have left for you is
hard, when the brassy years without it
have left an acid on the ease of purpose.
The woman faltered, admitting it
as she moved quickly to the window
and looked out where sunlight leaped
across the greenhouse glass. Breathless
she stood there, only to feel, to know, to see!
Her dress was hot, a straitjacket. The light was noble.
Nothing that was not past could ever be dull.
She turned back from the dazzling silence
and without a word ran into his arms.
Outside, the green drank the sun's deep good.

27

Cockerels, calabashes, girls he brought on board!
Mandolins, parakeets, a hunting-horn! He
was the king of the bay and knew what he was about.
He was the master of ungathered things.
He let the gunwhales rock, and sang
into the clouds of spray – ah, somehow he reclaimed them!
The instant death was over
more and more.
He splashed a parakeet to give one startling cry
that made a mandolin of the whole boat
as he stood braced against the sheets and little by little
drew out Leila to play her flute.
Harshly sweet in the wind the notes left her
and circled with the living water-wreaths.

33

Under the sun, dig up a king.
His whole retinue has been burnt like coal
to warm his afterlife. The
little jaws of dogs, even, lie as he suggested
at his feet. When the world is old
and nodding in its shawl of science,
and Prometheus's ray grows dim, and you and I,
Hafiz, are cold particles unknown, a
gem is to be made, they say, of suffering, to
glow and harden God knows where. Electric
sparks arc faintly. The damp
sizzles, the prophets sleep. The
story of the gem is what we tell our cat
at a drowsy firefall, disbelieving. Those were
the murdered. Pick and
spade are the best incantations.

37

Where can love, in this world, ever lodge?
Brisk angels might crisp up a mock sky crystalline
with it as their robes cut richly
through everything space has left behind,
an unimaginably silvery
dimension for that ice-blue crowd.
Think of the single ice and silver juggernaut
moving, singing, driving and
deepening, outside but into time. Which
is lover, which is loved? Is there a love window
in the universe, and are angel generations
talked down through it, a juggernaut answering like a trumpet?

53

In huge cups, in swags of stone, a fountain garden
fattened the snoring well-barbel'd carps. They lived
like dynasties, a shaded golden age. The garden,
bubbling and drowsing in a palm pocket,
dreamed, steamed, lay round its days
to hatch nearly nothing, to wind
about a carp-scale. His
algae kept the gardener happy. He thought
as he skimmed some, left some, with the sun flinging
watery light over his fingers, it would do.
He still hoped he would die there.
He always knew where the fish were,
his hand fed them, stroked the oldest back.
He lived like them in that great theatre
where the world is everything that is the case.

56

I saw a face in the waterfall
with ropy tears and great beard of glass
not steady, not vanishing either.
The crashing hieroglyphic
grew by what it was stripped of
like ants in armies.
Rocks made eyes and mouth, but whose?
There was no legend to tell us that.
Only the hooting of far-away ships
came up, and crickets in the grass. Into
the imagination a procession of scenes
hesitated, rejected by the melancholy
of a frozen mile-off regard
signalling without sense from its shroud.

64

They were building little houses of grass.
I cried. The radiation children would never
have children, or buy their houses of brick and glass. People
are running down the world's roads among
columns of smoke, with no more belongings than
a back can take. In the open
you must run, fire falls in a moment.
The burned ones lie on the common
after the roar has died. Their
shapes are a braille conducting
us silently from country to country
to country to country. Pale children
break the grass-blades in their hands.

69

Lovers linger by the harbour.
Evening draws its hood.
The world will do without
mages this hour, be covered
by a devoted look.
The shingle has a single
song, a gull steers in
by the half-built boat. The next
bride waits for summer,
turns in her bed to have
everybody's dreams. Houses
line the quayside with upper
windows lit. Below,
a mended sail shines clean.

71

Was that a writing angel
with its vast perhaps
plucking the reed-beds again? You never spoke,
as you never wrote. Clouds had the journey
fitfully jemmied open. Figures wakened
on rocks and stretched. You took a tissue
to that orange lipstick, shook hair as
black as seaweed in the pool. A pattern
a swirling moment gave went quickly. Coarse
fins were caught, flopped on boards. The woman
by the painter was your mother and the mother of
disoriented angels hooked on sense.

81

The night is over, the lark is singing,
the sages sit in full divan
in the anteroom of heaven,
the water bubbles, the pipe is sweet.
A pigeon calls over the marshes,
flaps across the anteroom glass.
Every wall's a window where
sages turn the innocent pages
and swivel the earth slowly around.
Their bell calls across the marshes.
The coffee-boy rows through to them,
still but a speck, and eye and ear
are waiting for the jugs to gleam,
the lifted oars to drop their diamonds,
the coffee song to cut the stillness.
Stillness of watched and watchers! Heaven
is twenty steps away. The lark
is in invisibility.
One sage slides back a whole glass wall,
the boat is moored, the glasses chink,
the steam comes in, the bell rings out,
the boy breaks bread and scatters it.
Pigeons, trembling, fill the marshes.
The sages sing the pigeon song
all that lingering forenoon,
forgetting earth, forgetting heaven.

82

We never thought we'd never die
but there it was at the moment of death,
the greatest fear we'd ever known.
We'd read of dragons – there they were,
or in the form of dragons, worse.
Winged leather, metal beat about us,
something stood with chains behind.
Electronic ozone stung,
parrots cut it shrieking. We'd
gone arthritic, sticklike, ashy,
took it all and tottered on.
We never thought we wouldn't burn
if that was what our lives had done,
but oh it was sharp all the same.
Writhing like grasses, gasping, clasping,
flaking out in beds of lava,
cockcrowed up to be rescorched,
the harpy beak and hackle red
above us like a flaming grid
we were to be spreadeagled on
we were spreadeagled over gulfs
so far below us we heard sighs
where nothing else could be exhaled
and even suffering was not seen.
Sultans who had dungeons once
– they say – stood there impaled.
We never thought we'd never weep
but that was so, oh that was so.
We never knew we'd have no more
to feel except one pain, one glow
memory blows us to, like coal.

86

Not in King's Regulations, to be in love.
Cosgrove I gave the flower to, joking, jumping down
the rocky terraces above Sidon, my heart bursting
as a village twilight spread its tent over us
and promontories swam far below
through goat-bells into an unearthly red.
He dribbled a ball through shrieking children and
they laughed at our bad Arabic, and the flower. To tell
the truth he knew no more of what I felt than of tomorrow.
Gallus, he cared little of that. I've not lost
his photograph. Yesterday, tomorrow
he slumbers in a word.

87

Cosgrove, Cosgrove, it is very dark.
The waves root like beasts.
Nothing wins – something breaks.
Wounded Crusaders howled in tents
before ruined Sidon Castle was built. Sandy
shores took keels like tigers and the
Saracen heroes raised their silver horns.
Afterwards, wailing of a mother
with ashes on her head.
Make do, make do!
History so fearfully
draws us backward
that to be gone
even as you are these thirty years is not to be
lost, although that later war's long done.

92

Angels with abacuses called their calculations
once, in an ancient scene of souls. They
shrug now, it's not calculable,
dive in pools, dry out half-human
with their wings on rocks and
let computers mass the injuries
let computers mess the injuries
let computers miss the injuries
let computers moss the injuries
let computers muss the injuries
of merely mortal times. Consequently
waters break on earth but not for them.
And those who see them in this
labouring place have shadows watching them,
not angels. It doesn't matter which.
When was our ACHTUNG MINEN ever their
concern, or their tears where our bodies were?

98

You came under my mosquito-net
many times, till you were posted far off.
I was innocent enough
to think the posting was accidental.
When you left, it was my studious
avoidance of you that said goodbye.
It was enough; the body, not the heart.
We'd our black comedy too –
the night you got up, on Mount Carmel,
with a dog's turd flattened on your shirt-front:
not funny, you said.

Well, it was all a really unwashable laundry
that finally had to be thrown away.

99

I dreaded stretcher-bearing,
my fingers would slip on the two sweat-soaked handles,
my muscles not used to the strain.
The easiest trip of all I don't forget,
in the desert, that dead officer
drained of blood, wasted away,
leg amputated at the thigh,
wrapped in a rough sheet, light as a child,
rolling from side to side of the canvas
with a faint terrible sound
as our feet stumbled through the sand.

100

The dead climb with us like the living to the edge.
The clouds sail and the air's washed blue. For you
and me, the life beyond that sages mention
is this life on a crag above
a line of breakers. Oh I can't speak
of that eternal break of white, only of
memories crowding in from human kind,
stealthily, brazenly, thankfully, stonily
into that other sea-cave
of my head. Down where the breaker was
closes, darkens, rises, foams, closes; crates
drift across, whirl round
in the ghost of a gale;

a shred of sailcloth
relic of a gale
that really blew slews to the resting-place
the long tide goes out
to leave it, bleaching on its bony rock.
I pick it from the stone,
Hafiz, to bind the leaves of my divan.

They told me that the night and day were all that I could see;
They told me that I had five senses to enclose me up,
And they enclosed my infinite brain into a narrow circle
And sunk my heart into the abyss, a red round globe hot-burning,
till all from life I was obliterated and erased.
– Blake

My fingers tremble when I touch the tapes.
Since we came back from earth, nothing's the same.
I tell you I hear that sea beyond the glass
throwing its useless music away in handfuls.
Once I angled a sweet chair to catch it.
I never even walk there now, far less
imagine vacant nature has a song.
Yet it's not vacant, wasn't that the point?
I must avoid questions, exclamations.
Keep your report formal, said the Council,
your evidence is for the memory-banks,
not for crude wonder or cruder appraisal.
I only report that nature is not the same.
And I report it within the spirit
of our resolve, which is indeed our duty,
to record whatever we have found to be,
to meditate on everything recorded,
and to record our meditations till
the plain figure of promised order appears.
I served, I took the oath: but my hand shakes
as I take up the damaged tapes and play them.

TAPE I: THE STONE
            ... had to go to the north shore
of the inland sea. There are six of us.
The stone we are to enter is well marked,

lies in a hollow and is as big as my fist.
Indeed the temptation to cup it, lift it, throw it
is strong. We resist. Whatever signals it gives
or is thought to give, only just not too faint
to rouse the interest of central monitors,
to us it's silent, like the stone it is.
The shrinking must be done by stages, but
even so it comes with a rush, doesn't
feel like shrinking. Rather it's the landscape
explodes upwards, outwards, the waves rise up
and loom like waterfalls, and where we stand
our stone blots out the light above us, a crag
pitted with caves and tunnels, immovable
yet somehow less solid. We climb, squeeze in
and one by one tramp through the galleries
till we have reached the designated cavern,
fan out on the dim rubbly floor, and wait.
We shrink again – accelerated this time.
The rubble's a mountain range, the shallow roof
a dark night sky in infinite soft distance.
The gallery we came by's like a black
hole in space. Off we go across the plain
into the new foothills. Have we moved at all?
I am not to speculate, only to explore
as commanded. I record it is harder now
to remember where we are, environment
tie-dyes memory into struggling patterns.
We always knew it stood to reason that
the smallest thing, seen close, would have some roughness,
but we could not envisage the sheer presence
of the blow-up, establishing its new world
each time, here, here, here: forget *there*, it says.
Dead though, all round, like a desert, and silent.
A desert in the middle of a stone!

– Erase the exclamation mark. Surprise
comes from old microstructure thinking.
We must stop that. We are beginning to learn
that where you are is what is, not less than
what is. 'You'd better not insult the Council,'
says Hlad. 'We're at the next diminishing-point.'
We sit together on the rocky slab,
join hands for safety, since the operation
must now be very fine, and suddenly
the six of us feel the whole desert-floor
strain outwards like a skin and burst in grains
of pale grey sand as large as asteroids.
We float to one, clamber aboard, and drift.
Space is like hard pure night traversed with flashes.
We must be near the atomic sub-structure.
I get a tenseness, Hazmon says vibration,
to Baltaz, with her keen ear, it seems music.
Kort stares at us, finds nothing, but 'Colder?'
he asks. My headache comes a little later.
But these are all expected signs; the Council
warned us the signals we are here to trace
(if they are signals) must be sending power
into a huge periphery, as our next stage
will tell. We brace ourselves for the last trip.
The asteroids boil up, swim out of sight,
we're plucked off into space by the force field
as cosmic dust and comets and star systems
grow out of nothing point by point of fire.
Our senders are directioning us now,
on slow shrinkdown, into a galaxy
that's soon wrapped round us with its long bright wings
and then expands as we contract until
it's tenuous and fair as haze. We're bound
for a smallish sort of sun, and planets

mushrooming about it, we don't move
but in our moving matrix we approach
the size that puts us in that system, lets
a too large world with rings go thundering past,
swells a speck of blue swirling with white
to a globe where millions of us could live,
white clouds and blue sky mount through us into
a strange protective canopy, and ground
of some sort rushes up to meet our feet
and scatters red and brown to far horizons
now the horizons of our sight. I'd say
the emanations here are like a source
of power; we've reached where we were sent; the new
blots out the old more strongly than before –
brown moor and yellow broom, a swooping bird
that clatters off some rocks with a wild cry,
and up there all those moving clouds, not fixed
as ours are in a chosen set but free
to drift and break as if they were not dead,
above a moorland where birds come and go
unchecked, wind shakes the easy heather bells
this way and that. In a dream we stand,
uncertain, abstracted, on the springy turf,
till 'Is there no Council here then?' asks Hlad,
and kills the spell. We tune in our receptors
but cannot unscramble the pervasive resonance.
Is it noise, and therefore not to be unscrambled,
or is it a simultaneity of signals,
or has their Council (if they have one) coded
their power for only equal power to crack?
Our expert, Tromro, gets to work on this.
Part of an unexpected answer comes,
not from Tromro, but from the landscape – it melts
at the edges like a photograph in flames,

throbs, re-forms, faces appear, a flare
of light on metal, swords ringing, a gold torque
filled with blood, the high whinny of horses,
dissolving back into a thrust of darkness.
It recomposes as a dusty plain
under a cloudless sky; we kick up dust;
we know now what we might have guessed: our time
and this world's time can never be in phase,
its images, its messages, its life
must come to us like an eternal present,
and by our very meagrest interfering
we trigger fragments of the vanished prints
but have no key to make the sequence clear.
Tromro will have to...

TAPE 2: THE EARTH
                           ... so confused.
Questions come thick and fast, we don't erase them.
This is most dangerous. The Council warned
any questioning was theirs alone.
What makes us disobey them? There – again!
A question and an exclamation, both.
Are we disintegrating, are we growing?
We've grown so small we can perhaps re-enter
places only the bewildered can be great in,
as we've heard books and tapes say were once ours,
histories back, in the red days of action.
Even to think of those days is a reproach.
I know that but I do not feel it. So?
So we are all able to change, nothing
can quite put down susceptibility,
not that I claim it as a virtue when
it stirs like wearing thorns: I record this,
with what relevance none of us can say.

And what I must record I must record:
the wind shrieks now across a desolation
of mirages, splintered castles, reed-beds,
a stork forms fishing, horsemen heavily
come together, canter with whips in fog,
a sullen mob, restrained, an open space
and though the picture never quite comes clear
we see the bellows at the huge fire, then
tongs drag out a red-hot iron throne,
a peasant's forced to sit on it, his head
pressed into a red-hot crown, his hand
clasped round a red-hot sceptre while the smoke
swirls over jeering breath: long live the king!
long live King Dózsa! and the rearing horses
foam at their jerked bits like an old frieze
till suddenly the whole scene snaps tight shut
and we're left staring at a sea of clouds.
We must be on some mountain-top at night,
with a full moon riding the black above
but tongues and limbs of mist stretching below,
mist or cloud we can hardly be sure,
cloud or sea we can hardly be sure
as the white masses die in distant grey
and hills might be the whales they loom like there,
but we imagine waves all round us, ride
on our mountain as moons ride their dark air.
We watch three climbers; a dog sniffs the rock;
one gaunt man stands apart, brooding intently
over the metamorphosis, we think
it's what he says we hear through the vague roar
of what must be big unseen mountain-streams.
'The emblem of a mind that feeds upon
infinity, that broods over the dark abyss,
intent to hear its voices issuing forth

to silent light in one continuous stream.'
The dog barks, and the scene strains out in white.
Facing us is a gigantic screen.
Scores of steamed-up cars are parked in rows.
A couple locked or twisting in a kiss
is silhouetted smoochily in each.
The summer desert air has stars, the screen
that no one looks at flickers crazily
and howls distorted sound at love-bites. It's
only a painted cat up there, grinning
as it rolls a bulldog in a hammock and
batters it, thinking it's a mouse. The film,
the sand, the erotic jalopies, fade
in a slow dim-out towards Arizona.
A bleached signpost like a cactus revolves
as the earth turns. Flashes, stripes of darkness
clatter up like jarring shutters: landscapes
come and go, at last one slows down, holds,
shimmering in a fine red autumn haze.
It seems a camp in time of war – barbed wire,
watchtowers, rows of huts, but also blocks
(too many surely to be bakeries)
with huge square chimneys – acrid smoke from one
drifts off over the stubble-fields. A train
of cattle-trucks has brought in new arrivals,
two thousand perhaps, men, women, children,
all ages, tired or apprehensive, joking,
reassuring, glad to stretch their legs,
filing into a hall with hooks for clothes.
A sign says BATH AND DISINFECTION ROOM.
Guards tell them to undress, help the worried,
the old, the sick; mothers help their children,
hush their crying; young couples hand in hand

smile at their nakedness, but some men sweat,
half-hide their fear, one moans, shakes like litmus.
In ten minutes all are ready, the guards
herd them to the farther door, unscrewing
the strange wheel that is its handle, and
all troop into the disinfection room,
some driven struggling, the last few screaming
as the thick oak door is screwed smoothly shut.
The beating on the panels mounts, and dies,
a thin susurrus filters through a while
like what I've read of spirits suffering,
but nothing is in my understanding.
I stare at Baltaz, who has clung to me
as if she was a woman of the earth,
and nothing on her features is not pain.
We have no pain, we cannot suffer pain.
I have nothing I can say to her but
'I saw no bath or cloth or soap or tap.
There was nothing but cement walls and floor,
and perforated columns of sheet-iron.
How do we know what earthmen do?' 'I know!'
she cries, 'I know what they do! Record it!
They make people into ash, turn babies
into smoke. Is that the message they've sent
out over all their puny universe?
Is that what scratched at our dish? The Council
sends explorers for a handful of that?
Dust, bones, gold rings, old women's rags? Take me
out of this earth, Erlkon, take us away.'
Before I can answer her, thunderclaps
bang sheets of rain across the fields, the camp
wavers, blotted out, is gone. We're left with
a heather moor like one we saw before,

and now it's hot: bees hum; the panic goes.
A butterfly's an epaulette on Kort's
thin shoulder, Hazmon laughs, holds out a twig
and the white creature flutters to it, Hlad
thinks this is childish but even he's benign.
Only Baltaz looks at the butterfly
as if she would cup its frailty for ever
against the eerie furnaces. She's changed.
I'm changing. I record this without comment.
For I don't want us recalled yet, not yet.
We must expose ourselves to it. To what? To that.
The Council will note I conserve questions.
Tromro has banks of information, Kort
spores, Hazmon has his films, Hlad and I the tapes,
Baltaz – Baltaz –
                   Sunset, in what I've read
is beauty, even glory, crowns the earth
with harmless fires. Colours of great fineness
from pearl to crimson to dark purple coast
and flush and doze and deepen and decay
in shapes we'd never give a name to in
a hundred days of watching them dissolve.
And now the stars come out above the hill.
It seems this is a world of change, where we,
observing, can scarcely fix the observed
and are unfixed ourselves. This solid hill
even as I speak is half transparent,
white walls and floors show through, we sink, the stars
are roof-lights in a large computer room.
The air is clear, the light even, the hall
vibrant as a heart. A screen we approach
switches itself on, flickers, fills with snow,
focuses to a powerful image
grainy and stark in grey-green, black and white.

Figures in domes – men, women – work and move.
They've left the earth, like seeds. Is it their moon,
or a near planet, or have they gone out
beyond their system into some neighbour
millimetre in the stone? – Tromro's job.
But now with an extreme concerted movement
the milling hundreds in one dome turn round
to face us, and the screen is scored with gestures
that make us catch our breath as they stretch out
arms seeming to implore us where we stand.
And every face flickers with white longing,
and some on knees, or drooping propped on friends,
or sunk with hair that sweeps the floor, some straight
and motionless in such a dignity,
some streaked with crying, all in such a case
we can but take as last or next to last
in desperation, and the time unknown
past, future, or the myriad-to-one
unthinkable and terrible present.
If it is now, we cannot save them; past,
what we feel must surely be pain; to come,
it's like a warning of all fate we've read
waits, though we must not believe it. The screen
scrambles in points of bluish light, goes blank.
We sit at consoles that go ghostly as
we search the data banks. Fragments of sound
clash out and shred to silence – *seventeen* –
leaning – a prominence – Christ yes man go –
solitaire et glacé – shoot from – eagles –
vstayot zarya vo mglye kholodnoy – burn –
done with Danny Deever – programme – Sturm und –
a gabble in a wilderness of wires,
an earth labouring in memories.
And soon we're in a void of echoes, faint

and more faint, merging with a rising wind
that stirs the greatest of the earth's huge seas.
It is all round us, boundless to the eye
although we know it is not boundless, blue
and blue-grey, steely, warmer green, green-black
with flecks of whipped-up white and longish swells
where hints of prussian browns, acid yellows,
glass pinks that only numbered charts could name
crosshatch the windy sharkskin; real sharkskin's
not far under, and tumbling whales; typhoon's
kingdom too. But now only a handful
of clouds is scattered through the morning sky.
The sun begins to walk on the Pacific.
And now we see and come down closer to
a speck that does not fit that emptiness.
A thousand miles from land, this black canoe,
long, broad, and strongly built, with fine high prow
much ornamented, and many oars, drives
forward steady across the zigzag sun-prints.
Tattoos as intricate as the prow-carving
stand out on the brown arms and backs and brows
as men who might be warriors bend and row,
yet seem explorers and not war-men, for their boat
has stores for major voyaging, animals,
children, and women slicing coconuts
and shaking back their long black shining hair,
offering rowers the fresh smiling milk.
The men are singing as they row, the chant
comes up, torn off in buffets of the wind,
returns in strength. By the gunwhale a cock crows.
Whatever far-off landfall is their goal,
known or unknown, or only hoped-for, they
have crossed dangerous immensity

like a field, and dangerous immensity
to come lies all about them without land:
their life is with the waves and wind, they move
forward in ordinary fortitude,
and someday they'll steer through that Southern Cross
they only steer by now.
                    There's a loud hum,
and swirling shadows fill the air. Hlad warns
he feels the signs are we must go. Tromro,
listening, confirms. It comes swifter than a blow.
The earth shrinks to a smaller point in space
than even the canoe was in its ocean.
A nebula like a riddle of flour
tempts us to shake out a few million worlds
in passing; fate might bake a thing from that.
Remagnification euphoria
is fiercer than we'd thought. We keep control
and wait for the next phase to...
END OF TAPE 2

I think not much was missing from that tape.
The phases came in order, without crisis.
We crept out of the rock, shot up, looked back
at what was now a stone again, ourselves
in our old scale of body, dune, and sea.
How uninteresting those dunes, that sea!
We made our report in a troubled confusion,
memories flashing between sentences
to make us falter, stare at the Council
as if they were an alien life-form. Hopeless –
they soon gave up politeness, froze us, said
our report was totally deplored, useless
to contemplate, ruinously incomplete;

feeling and action had besotted us;
our anti-brainwashing sessions had been
a clinic wasted; was earth such a paragon
or paradise or paradigm that we
lost our nature in a simple phasing? –
and they'd be training non-susceptibles
for a further expedition. What I suspect
is that susceptibility's a pearl of price,
now that I've heard the tapes again. It's true
the mission failed: we don't know whether earth
is sending or had sent a message or
was itself the message in dying it became,
though this too might be a real message sent
by the survivors gone to other stars.
We don't know even if there are survivors
now, for when is now? To me it seems
the virtue's in the questions, not the answers.
I think this fishbone's in the Council's throat,
for all their smoothing of the rule-book. It was
infinity the poet on the mountain said
the mind must feed on, which is very fine,
and I agree with it, but when we reach
the almost infinitely small and find
well-made extermination camps, nothing
seems infinite except cruelty, nothing
feeds the mind but processions to death.
Not true, not true. What is that infinite hope
that forces a canoe upon the waters,
infinite love in the woman comforting
her child at the mortal bathhouse door?
I think the break came when we showed the film
of Dózsa sizzling on his throne. 'Cut,' said
Council. 'We're not impressed by drops of sweat.
A xerox of the execution order

would suffice. Couldn't you see the man's been dead
this thousand thousand years?' 'No, he's not dead,'
I said. The Council stared as if I was
an alien life-form, which perhaps I am
now. How do I know whether Dózsa's dead?
Why don't the dead just disappear then? What
if the Council are all hallucinants
projected by hostile powers to keep us mild?
Who told who to tell us not to feel?
tell us love's wrong, leads to suffering?
hate's wrong, leads to fire and battlefields?
and questions above all are wrong, lead to
deflected meditation on the order
we wait to see: who says? What use is order
to a chained world under a painted sky?
If any order's there we'd break it like
a shell to let some living touch emerge.
Frail, frail, frail! Better than those pavilions
of molybdenum, demagnification banks
that rev for our successors! The cock crows still,
I hear it, praise it, on that southern sea.
The voyagers are out, the day is up,
and that's what we record last.
                                        We meet
in secret now, the six of us, from time
to time, and study how to change this life.
Baltaz has moved in with me; everything
seems like a great wave shining disclosed
travelling our planet's deadwater. Tromro
has taught us much; each frame of Hazmon's film
is burned into our minds; Hlad's tapes have noise
– every sound on earth – and mine have voice.
Baltaz is at her handbook: what we must do,
and when. But uncommunicative Kort's

our *wunderkind* (as earthmen say), he's made
a culture of the spores, they're growing at
their work not just of telling us what they are
but handing to our memories of earth
a life we'll make a source of life, begun
in purposes of rebuked pain and joy.

THE WORLD

I

I don't think it's not going onward,
though no one said it was a greyhound.
I don't accept we're wearing late.

I don't see the nothing some say anything
that's not in order comes to be found.
It may be nothing to be armour-plated.

I don't believe that what's been made
clutters the spirit. Let it be patented
and roll. It never terrorized

three ikon angels sitting at a table
in Moscow, luminous as a hologram
and blessing everything from holograms

to pliers at a dripping nail.
I don't believe it's not the wrench
of iron that let the body fall.

2

There was this unholy scuffle.
They felled the sober with the tipsy.
At last someone got pushed mildly

onto a breadknife. As he observed
in the ward, What's more, what's more,
just nobody's going to go there.

They did though. Even if which was which
was always a guessing-game, the case
meant the whole scene had bristles on.

Expressionless hardmen glittered. Sleepwalkers
jived. There was a dog. Before
the end of the evening a desire

for everything had returned, very
smoky it's true, but true. The sleeper
in the ward was the only one with nightmares.

3

Sometimes it swells like the echo of a passion
dying with paeans, not sighs. Who
knows the weight and list of its rebellions?

Underneath, underneath, underneath, underneath –
you think it beats in the age-old fashion,
even red, perhaps, like a pre-set strawberry

creeping below the crust? It's artistic
to have ordered impulses. To
think the world has makes you feel great.

Beyond the world, the slow-dying sun
flares out a signal fan, projecting
a million-mile arm in skinny hydrogen

to flutter it at our annals.
Coarse, knee-deep in years, we
go on counting, miss the vast unreason.

4

Technologies like dragonflies, the strange
to meet the strange; and at the heart
of things, who knows what is dependent?

Imagine anything the world could, it might
do; anything not to do, it would.
A plume of act flies as it spins by.

We saw the nettles in the ancient station.
The signalbox was like a windmill, haunted
by bats and autumn wasps. She

twirled a scarf through leaves. Remembrance
offered nothing, swam in our hands.
We're here. The past is not our home.

I don't think it's not being perfect
that brings the sorrows in, but being soon
beyond the force not to be powerless.

None of your jade suits, none of your gold-sewn princes! –
green-shelled spoonfuls of dust like coelacanths in tombs.
I want to be born again. Keep Tollund peat
for roses, boots, blazes. Men of Han, princesses,
yellowing demons and mummies, casket-crowders,
haunt off! There's never armour made
I'd pray to be preserved in. Don't preserve me!
Yesterday great Chou's ashes flew
in the wind over plain and river,
never resting or rusting, nothing
for an urn. Unknown he blows
like seed, is seed,
a little cinnamon of the millennium.
Let them roll away the black diorite
where millions shuffle past a husk.
What? Christ too like Chou could not be found.
In this strange January spring,
so mild the blackbirds go mad
singing in the morning above Anniesland,
I woke, I heard them, no one at my side,
but thought of you with the exhilaration
of that rising song where like them I scatter
and swoop in rings over the half-dark earth,
caught up in another life.

PARTICLE POEMS

I

The old old old old particle
smiled. 'I grant you I'm not beautiful,'
he said, 'but I've got charm.
It's charm that's led me where I am.'

Opened up his bosom, showed me a quark.
It gleamed. He grinned like a clam. 'Sort
of heart, really, though I've got four.
They're in orbit, and what for

is a good question, unless to pump up
charm. I know I must look a frump
– just fishing – but seriously
would you not say I'm easily

the nearest thing to doom and centrehood
you've ever been unable to preclude?
Cathedrals – oh, antiquities and slime,
knucklebones, teeth five feet long, signs

and wonders, auks, knuckledusters,
twangs from armchairs, waters
waiting to break, cells waiting to squeak,
a sniff of freesia, a book

of hours, and hours themselves like days
in love, and even nanoseconds raised
by charm to higher powers, wait
until I make them, and fade.'

Shot off – never showed his age.

2
The young particle screamed round the bend,
braked hard, broke.
His mother dozing in Manchuria
heard his last cry. A mare's ear twitched.
Dust, and dust, the wires sang.

3
Three particles lived in mystical union.
They made knife, fork, and spoon,
and earth, sea, and sky.
They made animal, vegetable, and mineral,
and faith, hope, and charity.
They made stop, caution, go,
and hickory, dickory, dock.
They made yolk, white, and shell,
and hook, line, and sinker.
They made pounds, shillings, and pence,
and Goneril, Regan, and Cordelia.
They made Shadrach, Meshach, and Abednego,
and game, set, and match.

A wandering particle kidnapped one of them,
and the two that were left made day and night,
and left and right, and right and wrong,
and black and white, and off and on,
but things were never quite the same,
and two will always yearn for three.
They're after you, or me.

4
Part particle and part idea, she
struggled through a throb of something.
A wheatear, or an ear of wheat?
How could she possibly know
beyond the shrill vibrations, sunny fibres, field?
What was the field but forces, surges?
To veins of green and veins of red
she was colour-blind. Well, she was blind.
But was she there at all –
when the wind ruffled that nest of growing things
and it took its course in the sun?

5
The particle that decided
got off its mark, but died.

6
Their mausoleum
is a frozen silent flak.
The fractured tracks,
photographed, docket
dead dogfights,
bursts of no malice.
Almost pure direction
points its stream,
deflected, detected.
Better than ogam
or cuneiform the tracer
of telling particles
fans out angrily
itself, itself, itself –

who we were
were here, here,
we died at the crossroads
or we defected
or we raced ahead
to be burnt out.
Faint paths hardly score,
yet shake the lens, end
in lucider mosaics
of theory. Go,
bid the soldiers shoot.

A HOME IN SPACE

Laid-back in orbit, they found their minds.
They found their minds were very clean and clear.
Clear crystals in swarms outside were their fireflies and larks.
Larks they were in lift-off, swallows in soaring.
Soaring metal is flight and nest together.
Together they must hatch.
Hatches let the welders out.
Out went the whitesuit riggers with frames as light as air.
Air was millions under lock and key.
Key-ins had computers wild on Saturday nights.
Nights, days, months, years they lived in space.
Space shone black in their eyes.
Eyes, hands, food-tubes, screens, lenses, keys were one.
One night – or day – or month – or year – they all –
all gathered at the panel and agreed –
agreed to cut communication with –
with the earth base – and it must be said they were –
were cool and clear as they dismantled the station and –

and gave their capsule such power that –
that they launched themselves outwards –
outwards in an impeccable trajectory, that band –
that band of tranquil defiers, not to plant any –
any home with roots but to keep a –
a voyaging generation voyaging, and as far –
as far as there would ever be a home in space –
space that needs time and time that needs life.

THE MOUTH

I saw a great mouth in space that fifty thousand angels could not fill
they ran shrieking from it as it grew and threw their coloured coats and flares
for lures among the stars while it advanced and swallowed the planets of the sun
one by one and then the sun

it rose and swayed the Milky Way collapsed into it like a poorly shuffled pack
deeper and deeper into darkness it brought darkness and what it blotted out
it grew drunk on to grinning-point with so much fire in its belly it roared
over its thankless hoard

for that was the new horror to hear it when it howled like a hungry scraped womb
and galaxies jampacked with glittering rayed-out million-year-old civilizations
were jumped like a handful of asteroids and sucked into tales of hell
for all they could tell

the Plough long gone the winding Dragon the Lyre the Balance the fading Chariotee
Aquarius with a loud cry Keel Stern and Sails in terrible rushing silence
and now white Sirius was black yellow Capella was black red Antares was black
and no lights ever came back

heavens and paradises popped like seaweed eternal laws were never seen again
angels' teeth were cosmic dust and cosmic dust was angels' teeth all's grist
to that dark mill where christs and godbearers were pulped with their domes ikons
vanes
their scrolls aeons and reigns

in Virgo the most evolved life there was was calm and watchful in its fiery coverts
the mouth had long been computed probable and plans had been laid and re-laid
the dense cluster of three thousand galaxies had made itself a force field
that would not know how to yield

the worlds of Virgo were not only inhabited but hyperinhabited they were all
one life and their force field was themselves they were a wall they shone they
stood
jehovahs and elohim are daguerreotypes to their movies they made universes
as poets make verses

in Virgo they did not underestimate the mouth they were the last star-gate and
goal
when they saw there were no other lights in the recesses of space and it was hard
to distinguish the shadow of the unsated mouth from the shadow of the dead
but its lips were blackest red

they gaped for Virgo with a scream they gaped for Virgo with a scream they
gaped for Virgo with a scream they gaped for Virgo with a scream they gaped for
Virgo with a scream they gaped at that great quiet gate

Amalthea

I took a book with me to Amalthea
but never turned a page. It weighed like lead.
I squatted with it like a grey image
malleted into the rock, listlessly
reading, staring, rereading listlessly
sentences that never came to anything.
My very memory lay paralysed
with everything else on that bent moon,
pulled down and dustbound, flattened, petrified
by gravitation, sweeping Jupiter's
more than half the sky with sentences
half-formed that never came to anything.
My tongue lay like a coil of iron, the planet
never heard a word. What did I say there?
My very memory is paralysed.
The book has gone too – I know how it began
but that first sentence never came to anything.
'The local train, with its three coaches, pulled up
at Newleigh Station at half-past four...'
The tons of pages never moved, my knees
were tombs, and though slow Jupiter slid past,
my memory of it is paralysed.
The stupid moon goes round. The local train,
with its three coaches pulled up at Newleigh Station
at half-past four, never comes to anything.
They rescued me with magnets, plucked me up
like dislocated yards of groaning mandrake.
The satellite engulfed the book in dust.

Io

The sulphur mines on Io were on strike
when we arrived. I can't say I'm surprised.
Seventy-five men had just been killed
in the fiercest eruption ever seen there.
I hardly recognized the grim volcano
with its rakish new centre and a leaning plume
two hundred miles high – like an ash tree,
someone said. Meanwhile the landscape burned,
not that it never burned before, but this
was roaring, sheeted, cruel. Empty
though not perfunctory funeral rites
had been performed; not a body was found.
The weird planetman's flute from friends in grief –
my god what a strange art it is, rising
so many million miles from home into
the raw thin cindery air – was the first sound
we heard when we stepped from the ship. We saw
the men huddled in knots, or walking slowly
with bent heads over the pumice beds, or still
and silent by the bank of the red lake.
The laser probes, the belts, the brilliant console
sat dark and motionless, crawled through by smoke.
Sulphur blew to choke the very soul.
We prospected beyond the lava-fields,
but the best sulphur's the most perilous.
The planetman must shoulder sorrow, great sacks
of pain, in places with no solace but
his own and what the winds and days may bring.

Europa

Boots and boats – in our bright orange gear
we were such an old-fashioned earthly lot
it seemed almost out of time-phase. We learned
or re-learned how to skate and ski, use snowshoes,
fish through ice-holes though not for fish. Soundings
and samples were our prey. We'd never grade
in years, far less in weeks, the infinite
play and glitter of watery Europa,
waters of crust ice, waters of deep ice,
waters of slush, of warm subcrustal springs,
waters of vapour, waters of water.
One day, and only one, we drilled right down
to something solid and so solid-hard
the drill-head screamed into the microphone
and broke, the film showed streaks of metal shards
whizzing across a band of basalt or
glimmery antediluvian turtle-shell
or cast-off titan miner's helmet or –
it must have been the metal scream that roused
our thought and fear and half desire we might
have had a living scream returned. Lightly
it sleeps, the imagination. On that smooth moon
men would be driven mad with many dreams,
hissing along the hill-less shining wastes,
or hearing the boat's engine chug the dark
apart, as if a curtain could be drawn
to let the living see even the dead
if they had once had life, if not that life.

Ganymede

Galileo would have been proud of Ganymede.
Who can call that marbled beauty dead?
Dark basins sweeping to a furrowed landfall,
gigantic bright-rayed craters, vestiges
and veils of ice and snow, black swirling grey,
grey veined with green, greens diffused in blues,
blue powdered into white: a king marble
rolled out, and set in place, from place to place.
We never landed, only photographed
and sent down probes from orbit; turbulence
on Jupiter was extreme, there was no lingering.
Is it beauty, or minerals, or knowledge
we take our expeditions for? What a question!
But is it What a question? Is it excitement,
or power, or understanding, or illumination
we take our expeditions for? Is it specimens,
or experiments, or spin-off, or fame, or evolution,
or necessity we take our expeditions for?
We are here, and our sons or our sons' sons
will be on Jupiter, and their sons' sons
at the star gate, leaving the fold of the sun.
I remember I drowsed off, dropped my notes,
with the image of Ganymede dancing before me.
They nudged me, smiling, said it was a judgement
for my wandering thoughts, what had got into me?
That satellite had iron and uranium.
We would be back. Well, that must be fine,
I teased them; had it gold, and asphodel?

Callisto

Scarred, cauterized, pocked and warty face:
you grin and gape and gawk and cock an ear
at us with craters, all blind, all deaf, all dumb,
toadback moon, brindled, brown and cold,
we plodded dryshod on your elephant-hide seas
and trundled gear from groove to groove, playing
the record of your past, imagining
the gross vales filled with unbombarded homes
they never had till we pitched nylon tents there:
radiation falling by the ton,
but days of meteorites long gone. Scatter
the yellow awnings, amaze the dust and ochre!
Frail and tough as flags we furnish out
the desolation. Even the greatest crater,
gouged as if a continent had struck it,
circled by rim on rim of ridges rippling
hundreds of miles over that slaty chaos,
cannot forbid our feet, our search, our songs.
I did not sing; the grave-like mounds and pits
reminded me of one grave long ago
on earth, when a high Lanarkshire wind
whipped out the tears men might be loath to show,
as if the autumn had a mercy I
could not give to myself, listening in shame
to the perfunctory priest and to my thoughts
that left us parted on a quarrel. These
memories, and love, go with the planetman
in duty and in hope from moon to moon.

THE MUMMY

(The Mummy [of Rameses II] *was met at Orly airport by Mme Saunier-Seïté.*
– News item, Sept. 1976)

– May I welcome Your Majesty to Paris.

– Mm.

– I hope the flight from Cairo was reasonable.

– Mmmmm.

– We have a germ-proof room at the Museum of Man
  where we trust Your Majesty will have peace and quiet.

– Unh-unh.

– I am sorry, but this is necessary.
  Your Majesty's person harbours a fungus.

– Fng fng's, hn?

– Well, it is something attacking your cells.
  Your Majesty is gently deteriorating
  after nearly four thousand years
  becalmed in masterly embalmment.
  We wish to save you from the worm.

– Wrm hrm! Mgh-mgh-mgh.

– Indeed I know it must be distressing
  to a pharaoh and a son of Ra,
  to the excavator of Abu Simbel
  that glorious temple in the rock,

to the perfecter of Karnak hall,
to the hammer of the Hittites,
to the colossus whose colossus
raised in red granite at holy Thebes
sixteen-men-high astounds the desert
shattered, as Your Majesty in life
shattered the kingdom and oppressed the poor
with such lavish grandeur and panache,
to Rameses, to Ozymandias,
to the Louis Quatorze of the Nile,
how bitter it must be to feel
a microbe eat your camphored bands.
But we are here to help Your Majesty.
We shall encourage you to unwind.
You have many useful years ahead.

– M' n'm 'z 'zym'ndias, kng'v kngz!

– Yes yes. Well, Shelley is dead now.
  He was not embalmed. He will not write
  about Your Majesty again.

– T't'nkh'm'n? H'tsh'ps't?
  'khn't'n? N'f'rt'ti? Mm? Mm?

– The hall of fame has many mansions.
  Your Majesty may rest assured
  your deeds will always be remembered.

– Youmm w'm'nn. B't'f'lll w'm'nnnn.
  No w'm'nnn f'r th'zndz y'rz.

– Your Majesty, what are you doing?

– Ng! Mm. Mhm. Mm? Mm? Mmmmm.

– Your Majesty, Your Majesty! You'll break your stitches!

– Fng st'chez fng's wrm hrm.

– I really hate to have to use
    a hypodermic on a mummy,
    but we cannot have you strain yourself.
    Remember your fungus, Your Majesty.

– Fng. *Zzzzzzz.*

– That's right.

– Aaaaaaaah.

INSTRUCTIONS TO AN ACTOR

Now, boy, remember this is the great scene.
You'll stand on a pedestal behind a curtain,
the curtain will be drawn, and then you don't move
for eighty lines; don't move, don't speak, don't breathe.
I'll stun them all out there, I'll scare them,
make them weep, but it depends on you.
I warn you eighty lines is a long time,
but you don't breathe, you're dead, you're dead,
you're a dead queen, a statue,
you're dead as stone, new-carved,
new-painted and the paint not dry
 – we'll get some red to keep your lip shining –
and you're a mature woman, you've got dignity,

some beauty still in middle age, and
you're kind and true, but you're dead,
your husband thinks you're dead,
the audience thinks you're dead,
and you don't breathe, boy, I say
you don't even blink for eighty lines,
if you blink you're out!
Fix your eye on something and keep watching it.
Practise when you get home. It can be done.
And you move at last – music's the cue.
When you hear a mysterious solemn jangle
of instruments, make yourself ready.
Five lines more, you can lift a hand.
It may tingle a bit, but lift it –
slow, slow –
O this is where I hit them
right between the eyes, I've got them now –
I'm making the dead walk –
you move a foot, slow, steady, down,
you guard your balance in case you're stiff,
you move, you step down, down from the pedestal,
control your skirt with one hand, the other hand
you now hold out –
O this will melt their hearts if nothing does –
to your husband who wronged you long ago
and hesitates in amazement
to believe you are alive.
Finally he embraces you, and there's nothing
I can give you to say, boy,
but you must show that you have forgiven him.
Forgiveness, that's the thing. It's like a second life.
I know you can do it. – Right then, shall we try?

MIGRAINE ATTACK

We had read about the reed-beds but went on
right through the night. With blades as sharp as that
you scarcely feel the cuts, and blood in darkness
is merely darkness. Oh there was moonlight
in fits and starts, but it confused us more
than it ever illuminated, as we kept moving
under the jagged filter of the forest ceiling –
whatever light there was made convicts of us,
frisked us, left us stumbling through our chains
of shadows. From our feet – shadows,
from our rifles – shadows, from branches –
shadows like bats and bats like shadows.
Sometimes the treetop mat was thick with mosses,
creepers, ancient nests, a stamping-ground
for upside-down explorers going to heaven:
we really saw them there, in our delirium,
riding on giant sloths, with their rags of clothes
and raddled hair streaming down to gravity.
They passed; the scrunts and scrogs passed; snakes passed;
eyes and beaks in bushes passed; a long wing passed;
the scuttlings and the slitherings and the roars
passed; time, even, as they passed, must have passed.
We were moving columns of sweat and crusted blood,
burrs, leaf-mould, mud, mosquitoes, map-cases
and a bandage or two as we leaned into it
to defeat it, and the wood grew grey
as it gave up and felt
the distant day, thinned out
to glades threaded by mist
sent from the unseen sun.
We shook ourselves like dogs
and tried a song.

WINTER

The year goes, the woods decay, and after,
many a summer dies. The swan
on Bingham's pond, a ghost, comes and goes.
It goes, and ice appears, it holds,
bears gulls that stand around surprised,
blinking in the heavy light, bears boys
when skates take over, the swan-white ice
glints only crystal beyond white. Even
dearest blue's not there, though poets would find it.
I find one stark scene
cut by evening cries, by warring air.
The muffled hiss of blades escapes into breath,
hangs with it a moment, fades off.
Fades off, goes, the scene, the voices fade,
the line of trees, the woods that fall, decay
and break, the dark comes down, the shouts
run off into it and disappear.
At last the lamps go too, when fog
drives monstrous down the dual carriageway
out to the west, and even in my room
and on this paper I do not know
about that grey dead pane
of ice that sees nothing and that nothing sees.

THE COALS

Before my mother's hysterectomy
she cried, and told me she must never bring
coals in from the cellar outside the house,
someone must do it for her. The thing itself
I knew was nothing, it was the thought

of that dependence. Her tears shocked me
like a blow. As once she had been taught,
I was taught self-reliance, discipline,
which is both good and bad. You get things done,
you feel you keep the waste and darkness back
by acts and acts and acts and acts and acts,
bridling if someone tells you this is vain,
learning at last in pain. Hardest of all
is to forgive yourself for things undone,
guilt that can poison life – away with it,
you say, and it is loath to go away.
I learned both love and joy in a hard school
and treasure them like the fierce salvage of
some wreck that has been built to look like stone
and stand, though it did not, a thousand years.

GRENDEL

It is being nearly human
gives me this spectacular darkness.
The light does not know what to do with me.
I rise like mist and I go down like water.
I saw them soused with wine behind their windows.
I watched them making love, twisting like snakes.
I heard a blind man pick the strings, and sing.
There are torches everywhere, there are faces
swimming in shine and sweat and beer and grins and greed.
There are tapers confusing the stacked spears.
There are queens on their knees at idols, crosses, lamps.
There are handstand clowns knocked headlong by maudlin heroes.
There are candles in the sleazy bowers, the whores
sleep all day with mice across their feet.

The slung warhorn gleams in the drizzle,
the horses shift their hooves and shiver.
It is all a pestilence, life within life
and movement within movement, lips meeting,
grooming of mares, roofs plated with gold,
hunted pelts laid on kings,
neck-veins bursting from greasy torques,
pouches of coins gamed off, slaves and outlaws
eating hailstones under heaven.
Who would be a man? Who would be the winter sparrow
that flies at night by mistake into a lighted hall
and flutters the length of it in zigzag panic,
dazed and terrified by the heat and noise and smoke,
the drink-fumes and the oaths, the guttering flames,
feast-bones thrown to a snarl of wolfhounds,
flash of swords in sodden sorry quarrels,
till at last he sees the other door
and skims out in relief and joy
into the stormy dark?
– Black grove, black lake, black sky,
no shoe or keel or wing undoes your stillness
as I plod through the fens and prowl
in my own place and sometimes stand many hours, as now,
above those unreflecting waters, reflecting as I can
on men, and on their hideous clamorous brilliance
that beats the ravens' beaks into the ground
and douses a million funeral pyres.

JACK LONDON IN HEAVEN

Part the clouds, let me look down.
Oh god that earth. A breeze comes from the sea
and humpback fogs blanch off to blindness, the sun
hits Frisco, it shines solid up to heaven.
I can't bear not to see a brisk day on the Bay,
it drives me out of my mind but I can't bear
not to watch the choppy waters, Israfel.
I got a sea-eagle once to come up here
screaming and turn a prayer-wheel or two
with angry buffets till the sharpshooters
sent him to hell, and I groaned,
grew dark with disfavour. – What,
I should pray now? For these thoughts?
Here are some more. I was up at four
for psalms, shawms, smarms, salaams, yessirs, yesmaams,
felt-tipped hosannas melting into mist,
a mushroom high, an elation of vapours,
a downpour of dumpy amens. Azazel,
I am sick of fireflies. It's a dumb joss.
– You know I'm a spoilt angel? What happens to us?
I'm not so bright – or bright, perhaps. God knows!
They almost let me fall through heaven craning
to see sunshine dappling the heaving gunmetal
of the Oakland Estuary – the crawl, the swell, the crests
I could pull up to touch and wet my hands
let down a moment into time and space.
How long will they allow me to remember
as I pick the cloud-rack apart and peer?
The estuary, Israfel, the glittery estuary, August '96!
My last examination has scratched to a finish,
I'm rushing to the door, whooping and squawking,
I dance down the steps, throw my hat in the air
as the dusty invigilator frowns, gathers in

that furious harvest of four months' cramming,
nineteen hours a day – my vigils, Azazel,
my holy vigils – the oyster-pirate hammering
at the gates of the state university.
It's enough. I got in. But at that time
I took a boat out on the ebb
to be alone where no book ever was.
I scudded dreaming through the creamy rings
of light and water, followed the shore
and thought of earth and heaven and myself
till I saw a shipyard I knew, and the delta rushes
and the weeds and the tin wharves, and smelt the ropes
and some tobacco-smoke, and longed for company.
  – Evensong? I'm not coming to evensong.
Get off, get away. Go on, sing for your supper!
Bloody angels! – So I sailed in, made fast,
and there was Charley, and Liz, and Billy and Joe, and Dutch
– that desperate handsome godlike drunken man –
old friends, Azazel, old friends that clambered over me
and sang and wept and filled me with whisky and beer
brought teetering across the railroad tracks
all that long noon.
They would have kept me there, oh, for ever
but I could see the blue through the open door,
that blue, my sea, and they knew
I had to be away, and got me stumbling down the wharf steps
into a good salmon boat, with charcoal and a brazier
and coffee and a pot and a pan and a fresh-caught fish
and cast me off into a stiff wind.
I tell you, Israfel, the sea was white
and half of it was in my boat
and with my sail set hard like a board.
Everything whipped and cracked

in pure green glory as
I stood braced at the mast
and roared out 'Shenandoah'.
Did Odysseus get to heaven?
I came down to earth, at Antioch,
sobered in the sunset shadows, tied up
alongside a potato sloop, had friends
aboard there too, who sizzled my fish for me
and gave me stew and crusty bread and claret,
claret in great pint mugs, and wrapped me in blankets
warmer and softer than the clouds of heaven.
What did we not talk of as we smoked,
sea-tales Odysseus might have known,
under the same night wind, the same wild rigging.
– Azazel, I must get down there!
I am a wasting shade, I am drifting and dying
by these creeping streams. If you are my friend,
tell them my trouble. Tell them
they cannot make me a heaven
like the tide-race and the tiller
and a broken-nailed hand
and the shrouds of Frisco.

Cinquevalli is falling, falling.
The shining trapeze kicks and flirts free,
solo performer at last.
The sawdust puffs up with a thump,
settles on a tangle of broken limbs.
St Petersburg screams and leans.
His pulse flickers with the gas-jets. He lives.

Cinquevalli has a therapy.
In his hospital bed, in his hospital chair
he holds a ball, lightly, lets it roll round his hand,
or grips it tight, gauging its weight and resistance,
begins to balance it, to feel its life attached to his
by will and knowledge, invisible strings
that only he can see. He throws it
from hand to hand, always different,
always the same, always
different, always the
same.
His muscles learn to think, his arms grow very strong.

Cinquevalli in sepia
looks at me from an old postcard: bundle of enigmas.
Half faun, half military man; almond eyes, curly hair,
conventional moustache; tights, and a tunic loaded
with embroideries, tassels, chains, fringes; hand on hip
with a large signet-ring winking at the camera
but a bull neck and shoulders and a cannon-ball
at his elbow as he stands by the posing pedestal;
half reluctant, half truculent,
half handsome, half absurd,
but let me see you forget him: not to be done.

Cinquevalli is a juggler.
In a thousand theatres, in every continent,
he is the best, the greatest. After eight years perfecting
he can balance one billiard ball on another billiard ball
on top of a cue on top of a third billiard ball
in a wine-glass held in his mouth. To those
who say the balls are waxed, or flattened,
he patiently explains the trick will only work
because the spheres are absolutely true.
There is no deception in him. He is true.

Cinquevalli is juggling with a bowler,
a walking-stick, a cigar, and a coin.
Who foresees? How to please.
The last time round, the bowler
flies to his head, the stick sticks in his hand,
the cigar jumps into his mouth, the coin
lands on his foot – ah, but
is kicked into his eye
and held there as the miraculous monocle
without which the portrait would be incomplete.

Cinquevalli is practising.
He sits in his dressing-room talking to some friends,
at the same time writing a letter with one hand
and with the other juggling four balls.
His friends think of demons, but
'You could all do this,' he says,
sealing the letter with a billiard ball.

Cinquevalli is on the high wire in Odessa.
The roof cracks, he is falling, falling
into the audience, a woman breaks his fall,
he cracks her like a flea, but lives.

Cinquevalli broods in his armchair in Brixton Road.
He reads in the paper about the shells whining
at Passchendaele, imagines the mud and the dead.
He goes to the window and wonders through that dark evening
what is happening in Poland where he was born.
His neighbours call him a German spy.
'Kestner, Paul Kestner, that's his name!'
'Keep Kestner out of the British music-hall!'
He frowns; it is cold; his fingers seem stiff and old.

Cinquevalli tosses up a plate of soup
and twirls it on his forefinger; not a drop spills.
He laughs, and well may he laugh
who can do that. The astonished table
breathe again, laugh too, think the world
a spinning thing that spills, for a moment, no drop.

Cinquevalli's coffin sways through Brixton
only a few months before the Armistice.
Like some trick they cannot get off the ground
it seems to burden the shuffling bearers, all their arms
cross-juggle that displaced person, that man
of balance, of strength, of delights and marvels,
in his unsteady box at last into the earth.

The fog rolled through the valley in great force.
The bridge was down, they'd never leave that night.
Once the girl got sticks and made a fire
it was quite snug. McAndrew had his flask.
The old organ took Curly's arpeggios
very decently, and there was trout for supper.
Poor Black thought he heard gunfire, but
he was always hearing things. Owls, yes,
but any guns were in the next valley. Niven
brushed out her hair with her back to the fire
as if she'd always lived there. No one lived there
except the dotty caretaker, and he'd gone
to bed. Rod was telling stories about fog
in that ursa major voice of his, when
Black said 'Listen!' and there were four smart taps
on the french window. The girl swore afterwards
she'd seen a shape, but it was only fog –
the snow would have left footprints. Branches?
Nothing was near. Bats then? Scrabbling
was not the sound, it was knuckles on glass.
'I tell you –' Black began, but the macabre
is of limited interest, like far-off gunfire,
and this is not a ghost story. Curly thought
the glass was cracking in unaccustomed heat
from the fire; Rod said it was the organ.
They laughed, and wrestled on the sheepskin.
At first light they all left for the next valley,
blowing on their hands. 'Snowshoes!' the girl cried,
but there was no one listening, in that wind.
So they found out nothing of the stranger
who tapped the glass at dark and disappeared.
They missed the code. They walked right into it.

HEAVEN

We have seen too many films
to be bowled over by many mansions,
but still, there it was: big, mostly bright,
crowding off as far as eye could see,
a palimpsest of saved burrows and pinnacles
in so many dimensions it seemed insubstantial,
yet busy with colour, smells, cries, stripes of light
like an old bazaar.
Bizarre! And keys at the gate! Incredible! Rings of them,
ancient, made of metal, for each arriver –
and no instructions to find your own place.
We have had too many nightmares
not to know that winding drive
that grows darker and darker
overhung with rhododendrons.
Shaking, we follow it
to the black, mossed porch.
The house is derelict.
We tiptoe up the stair
to the last room
with the last key
and get it to growl
round in its hole
and let us push into
paradise, paradise
please, if we may.

Through the storm he walked before he gave his sermon.
The sails were whipped to shreds. He took a turn.
There was hardly any air not dense with spray,
they choked as they half saw him out there
going or coming, who knows, through the sea-lumps.
His face was like a sheet of lightning. 'Beside him,
his injured arm in a sling, was Red Nelson,
his sou'wester gone and his fair hair plastered in wet,
wind-blown ringlets about his face. His whole attitude
breathed indomitability, courage, strength.
It seemed almost as though the divine
were blazing forth from him.' They shipped water,
baled, shipped water, baled, baled, baled.
Things blew themselves out. They tottered to shore,
too busy to see him back on board,
though he'd baled, he told them. There was no sermon.
They dried their rags on stones, he kept his on,
sitting a little apart, his sou'wester gone
and his fair hair plastered in wet, wind-blown
ringlets about his face. His whole attitude breathed
indomitability, courage, strength. It seemed
almost as though the divine were blazing forth from him.

They asked me to write this faithfully.
I do, and yet I am not sure that I do.
Sometimes I frown at what the pen has said.
My understanding breaks in waves, dissolves.
I am tired of walking on the sea.
Give me ice or vapour, terra firma,
some change that is a change not a betrayal.
Water would be water even with footprints
soldered to it in characters of fire
– as they were that day – God knows – as they were!

SONNETS FROM SCOTLAND

O Wechsel der Zeiten! Du Hoffnung des Volks!
– Brecht

Slate

There is no beginning. We saw Lewis
laid down, when there was not much but thunder
and volcanic fires; watched long seas plunder
faults; laughed as Staffa cooled. Drumlins blue as
bruises were grated off like nutmegs; bens,
and a great glen, gave a rough back we like
to think the ages must streak, surely strike,
seldom stroke, but raised and shaken, with tens
of thousands of rains, blizzards, sea-poundings
shouldered off into night and memory.
Memory of men! That was to come. Great
in their empty hunger these surroundings
threw walls to the sky, the sorry glory
of a rainbow. Their heels kicked flint, chalk, slate.

Carboniferous
For I.R.

Diving in the warm seas around Bearsden,
cased in our superchitin scuba-gear,
we found a world so wonderfully clear
it seemed a heaven given there and then.
Hardly! *Et in Arcadia*, said the shark,
ego. We stumbled on a nest of them.
How could bright water that hid nothing stem
our ancient shudder? They themselves were dark,
but all we saw was the unsinister
ferocious tenderness of mating shapes,
a raking love that scoured their skin to shreds.
We feared instead the force that could inter
such life and joy, in fossil clays, for apes
and men to haul into their teeming heads.

Post-Glacial

The glaciers melt slowly in the sun.
The ice groans as it shrinks back to the pole.
Loud splits and cracks send shudders through the shoal
of herring struggling northwards, but they run
steadily on into the unknown roads
and the whole stream of life runs with them. Brown
islands hump up in the white of land, down
in the valleys a fresh drained greenness loads
fields like a world first seen, and when mild rains
drive back the blizzards, a new world it is
of grain that thrusts its frenzied spikes, and trees
whose roots race under the stamped-out remains
of nomad Grampian fires. Immensities
are mind, not ice, as the bright straths unfreeze.

In Argyll
    For A.R.

We found the poet's skull on the machair.
It must have bobbed ashore from that shipwreck
where the winged men went down in rolling dreck
of icebound webs, oars, oaths, armour, blind air.
It watches westward still; dry, white as chalk,
perfect at last, in silence and at rest.
Far off, he sang of Nineveh the blest,
incised his tablets, stalked the dhow-bright dock.
Now he needs neither claws nor tongue to tell
of things undying. Hebridean light
fills the translucent bone-domes. Nothing brings
the savage brain back to its empty shell,
distracted by the shouts, the reefs, the night,
fighting sleet to fix the tilt of its wings.

The Ring of Brodgar

'If those stones could speak –' Do not wish too loud.
They can, they do, they will. No voice is lost.
Your meanest guilts are bonded in like frost.
Your fearsome sweat will rise and leave its shroud.
I well recall the timeprint of the Ring
of Brodgar we discovered, white with dust
in twenty-second-century distrust
of truth, but dustable, with truths to bring
into the freer ages, as it did.
A thin groan fought the wind that tugged the stones.
It filled an auditorium with pain.
Long was the sacrifice. Pity ran, hid.
Once they heard the splintering of the bones
they switched the playback off, in vain, in vain.

Silva Caledonia

The darkness deepens, and the woods are long.
We shall never see any stars. We thought
we heard a horn a while back, faintly brought
through barks and howls, the nearest to a song
you ever heard in these grey dripping glens.
But if there were hunters, we saw not one.
Are there bears? Mist. Wolves? Peat. Is there a sun?
Where are the eyes that should peer from those dens?
Marsh-lights, yes, mushroom-banks, leaf-mould, rank ferns,
and up above, a sense of wings, of flight,
of clattering, of calls through fog. Yet men,
going about invisible concerns,
are here, and our immoderate delight
waits to see them, and hear them speak, again.

Pilate at Fortingall

A Latin harsh with Aramaicisms
poured from his lips incessantly; it made
no sense, for surely he was mad. The glade
of birches shamed his rags, in paroxysms
he stumbled, toga'd, furred, blear, brittle, grey.
They told us he sat here beneath the yew
even in downpours; ate dog-scraps. Crows flew
from prehistoric stone to stone all day.
'See him now.' He crawled to the cattle-trough
at dusk, jumbled the water till it sloshed
and spilled into the hoof-mush in blue strands,
slapped with useless despair each sodden cuff,
and washed his hands, and watched his hands, and washed
his hands, and watched his hands, and washed his hands.

The Mirror

There is a mirror only we can see.
It hangs in time and not in space. The day
goes down in it without ember or ray
and the newborn climb through it to be free.
The multitudes of the world cannot know
they are reflected there; like glass they lie
in glass, shadows in shade, they could not cry
in airless wastes but that is where they go.
We cloud it, but it pulses like a gem,
it must have caught a range of energies
from the dead. We breathe again; nothing shows.
Back in space, *ubi solitudinem*
faciunt pacem appellant. Ages
drum-tap the flattened homes and slaughtered rows.

The Picts

Names as from outer space, names without roots:
Bes, son of Nanammovvezz; Bliesblituth
that wild buffoon throned in an oaken booth;
wary Edarnon; brilliant Usconbuts;
Canutulachama who read the stars.
Where their fame flashed from, went to, is unknown.
The terror of their warriors is known,
naked, tattooed on every part (the hairs
of the groin are shaved on greatest fighters,
the fine bone needle dipped in dark-blue woad
rings the flesh with tender quick assurance:
he is *diuperr cartait*, rich pin; writers
like us regain mere pain on that blue road,
they think honour comes with the endurance).

142

Colloquy in Glaschu

God but *le son du cor*, Columba sighed
to Kentigern, *est triste au fond silvarum*!
Frater, said Kentigern, I see no harm.
J'aime le son du cor, when day has died,
deep in the *bois*, and oystercatchers rise
before the fowler as he trudges home
and *sermo lupi* loosens the grey loam.
À *l'horizon lointain* is paradise,
abest silentium, le cor éclate –
– *et meurt*, Columba mused, but Kentigern
replied, *renaît et se prolonge*. The cell
is filled with song. Outside, *puer cantat*.
Veni venator sings the gallus kern.
The saints dip startled cups in Mungo's well.

Memento

over the cliff-top and into the mist
across the heather and down to the peat
here with the sheep and where with the peeweet
through the stubble and by the pheasant's tryst
above the pines and past the northern lights
along the voe and out to meet the ice
among the stacks and round their kreidekreis
in summer lightning and beneath white nights
behind the haar and in front of the tower
beyond the moor and against writ and ring
below the mort-gate and outwith all kind
under the hill and at the boskless bower
over the hills and far away to bring
over the hills and far away to mind

Matthew Paris

'North and then north and north again we sailed,
not that God is in the north or the south
but that the north is great and strange, a mouth
of baleen filtering the unknown, veiled
spoutings and sportings, curtains of white cold.
I made a map, I made a map of it.
Here I have bristly Scotland, almost split
in two, what sea-lochs and rough marches, old
forts, new courts, when Alexander their king
is dead will they live in love and peace, get
bearings, trace mountains, count stars, take capes, straits
in their stride as well as crop and shop, bring
luck home? *Pelagus vastissimum et
invium*, their element, my margin, waits.'

At Stirling Castle, 1507

Damian, D'Amiens, Damiano –
we never found out his true name, but there
he crouched, swarthy, and slowly sawed the air
with large strapped-on bat-membrane wings. Below
the battlements, a crowd prepared to jeer.
He frowned, moved back, and then with quick crow struts
ran forward, flapping strongly, whistling cuts
from the grey heavy space with his black gear
and on a huge spring and a cry was out
beating into vacancy, three, four, five,
till the crawling scaly Forth and the rocks
and the upturned heads replaced that steel shout
of sky he had replied to – left alive,
and not the last key snapped from high hard locks.

Thomas Young, M.A. (St Andrews)

For J.C.B.

'Yes, I taught Milton. He was a sharp boy.
He never understood predestination,
but then who does, within the English nation?
I did my best to let him see what joy
there must be in observing the damnation
of those whom God makes truly reprobate:
the fair percentage does not decreate
heaven, but gives all angels the elation
they are justly decreed to have deserved.
We took a short tour up to Auchterarder,
where there are strong sound sergeants of the creed,
but John could only ask how God was served
by those who neither stand nor wait, their ardour
rabid (he said) to expunge virtue's seed?'

Lady Grange on St Kilda

'They say I'm mad, but who would not be mad
on Hirta, when the winter raves along
the bay and howls through my stone hut, so strong
they thought I was and so I am, so bad
they thought I was and beat me black and blue
and banished me, my mouth of bloody teeth
and banished me to live and cry beneath
the shriek of sea-birds, and eight children too
we had, my lord, though I know what you are,
sleekit Jacobite, showed you up, you bitch,
and screamed outside your close at Niddry's Wynd,
until you set your men on me, and far
I went from every friend and solace, which
was cruel, out of mind, out of my mind.'

Theory of the Earth

James Hutton that true son of fire who said
to Burns 'Aye, man, the rocks melt wi the sun'
was sure the age of reason's time was done:
what but imagination could have read
granite boulders back to their molten roots?
And how far back was back, and how far on
would basalt still be basalt, iron iron?
Would second seas re-drown the fossil brutes?
'We find no vestige of a beginning,
no prospect of an end.' They died almost
together, poet and geologist,
and lie in wait for hilltop buoys to ring,
or aw the seas gang dry and Scotland's coast
dissolve in crinkled sand and pungent mist.

Poe in Glasgow

The sun beat on the Moby-Dick-browed boy.
It was a day to haunt the Broomielaw.
The smell of tar, the slap of water, draw
his heart out from the wharf in awe and joy.
Oh, not Virginia, not Liverpool –
and not the Isle of Dogs or Greenwich Reach –
but something through the masts – a blue – a beach –
an inland gorge of rivers green and cool.
'Wake up!' a sailor coiled with bright rope cried
and almost knocked him off his feet, making
towards his ship. 'You want to serve your time
as cabin-boy's assistant, eh?' The ride
and creak of wood comes home, testing, shaking.
'Where to?' He laughed. 'To Arnheim, boy, Arnheim!'

De Quincey in Glasgow

Twelve thousand drops of laudanum a day
kept him from shrieking. Wrapped in a duffle
buttoned to the neck, he made his shuffle,
door, table, window, table, door, bed, lay
on bed, sighed, groaned, jumped from bed, sat and wrote
till the table was white with pages, rang
for his landlady, ordered mutton, sang
to himself with pharmacies in his throat.
When afternoons grew late, he feared and longed
for dusk. In that high room in Rottenrow
he looks out east to the Necropolis.
Its crowded tombs rise jostling, living, thronged
with shadows, and the granite-bloodying glow
flares on the dripping bronze of a used kris.

Peter Guthrie Tait, Topologist

Leith dock's lashed spars roped the young heart of Tait.
What made gales tighten, not undo, each knot?
Nothing's more dazzling than a ravelling plot.
Stubby crisscrossing fingers fixed the freight
so fast he started sketching on the spot.
The mathematics of the twisted state
uncoiled its waiting elegances, straight.
Old liquid chains that strung the gorgeous tot
God spliced the mainbrace with, put on the slate,
and sent creation reeling from, clutched hot
as caustic on Tait's brain when he strolled late
along the links and saw the stars had got
such gouts and knots of well-tied fire the mate
must sail out whistling to his stormy lot.

G.M. Hopkins in Glasgow
For J.A.M.R.

Earnestly nervous yet forthright, melted
by bulk and warmth and unimposed rough grace,
he lit a ready fuse from face to face
of Irish Glasgow. Dark tough tight-belted
drunken Fenian poor ex-Ulstermen
crouched round a brazier like a burning bush
and lurched into his soul with such a push
that British angels blanched in mid-amen
to see their soldier stumble like a Red.
Industry's pauperism singed his creed.
He blessed them, frowned, beat on his hands. The load
of coal-black darkness clattering on his head
half-crushed, half-fed the bluely burning need
that trudged him back along North Woodside Road.

1893
For P. McC.

A Slav philosopher in Stronachlachar:
Vladimir Solovyov looked down the loch.
The sun was shimmering on birk and sauch.
'This beats the fishy vennels of St Machar,'
he said, and added, 'Inversnaid tomorrow!'
A boatman rowing to him from infinity
turned out to be a boatwoman. 'Divinity!'
he cried, 'shake back your hair, and shake back sorrow!'
The boat was grounded, she walked past him singing.
To her, he was a man of forty, reading.
Within him the words mounted: 'Sing for me,
dancing like Wisdom before the Lord, bringing
your mazy unknown waters with you, seeding
the Northern Lights and churning up the sea!'

The Ticket

'There are two rivers: how can a drop go
from one stream to the next?' Gurdjieff was asked.
The unflummoxable master stretched, basked.
'It must buy a ticket,' he said. A row
of demons dragged the Inaccessible
Pinnacle through the centre of Glasgow,
barking out sweaty orders, pledged to show
it was bloody juggernaut-time, able
to jam shrieking children under crashed spires.
But soon that place began to recompose,
the film ran back, the walls stood, the cries died,
the demons faded to familiar fires.
In New York, Gurdjieff changed his caftan, chose
a grape, sat, smiled. 'They never paid their ride.'

North Africa

Why did the poets come to the desert?
They learned the meaning of an oasis,
the meaning of heat, fellahin's phrases,
tents behind the khamsin-blasted dannert.
We watched MacLean at the Ruweisat Ridge
giving a piercing look as he passed by
the fly-buzzed grey-faced dead; swivelled our eye
west through tank-strewn dune and strafed-out village
with Henderson; and Hay saw Bizerta
burn; Garioch was taken at Tobruk,
parched *Kriegsgefangener*, calm, reading *Shveik*;
Morgan ate sand, slept sand at El Ballah
while gangrened limbs dropped in the pail; Farouk
fed Fraser memorandums like a shrike.

Caledonian Antisyzygy

– Knock knock. – Who's there? – Doctor. – Doctor Who? – No,
just Doctor. – What's up Doc? – Stop, that's all cock.
– O.K. – Knock knock. – Who's there? – Doctor Who. – Doc-
tor Who who? – Doctor, who's a silly schmo?
– Right. Out! – Aw. – Well, last chance, come on. – Knock knock.
– Who's there? – Doctor Jekyll. – Doctor Jekyll
who? – Doctor, 'd ye kill Mr Hyde? – Pig-swill!
Nada! Rubbish! Lies! Garbage! Never! Schlock!
– Calm down, your turn. – Knock knock. – Who's there? – Doctor
Knox. – Doctor Knox who? – Doctor Knocks Box Talks.
Claims T.V. Favours Grim Duo, Burke, Hare.
– Right, join hands. Make sure the door is locked, or
nothing will happen. – Dark yet? – Cover clocks.
– Knock. – Listen! – Is there anybody there?

Travellers (1)

The universe is like a trampoline.
We chose a springy clump near Arrochar
and with the first jump shot past Barnard's Star.
The universe is like a tambourine.
We clashed a brace of planets as we swung
some rolling unknown ringing system up
above our heads, and kicked it too. To sup,
sleep, recoup, we dropped to the House of Tongue.
The universe is like a trampoline.
Tongue threw us into a satellite bank.
We photographed a mole; a broch; the moon.
The universe is like a tambourine.
We stretched out, shook Saturn, its janglings sank
and leapt till it was neither night nor noon.

Travellers (2)

As it was neither night nor noon, we mused
a bit, dissolved ourselves a bit, took stock,
folded the play away and turned the lock.
Exhilarated travellers unused
to feeling blank can love the nescience
of a stilled moment. Undenied the time,
a lingering, a parasol, a lime.
There is no happiness in prescience,
and there is no regret in happiness.
A coast swept out in headlands and was lost.
And there we could have left the thought unthought
or hope undrafted, but that a bright press
of lights showed where a distant liner crossed.
Its horn blew through us, urgent, deep, unsought.

Seferis on Eigg

The isles of Scotland! the isles of Scotland!
But Byron sang elsewhere; loved, died elsewhere.
Seferis stiffly cupped warm blue May air
and slowly sifted it from hand to hand.
It was good and Greek. Amazed to find it,
he thought the dancing sea, the larks, the boats
spoke out as clear as from Aegean throats.
What else there was – he might half-unwind it.
One day he visited the silent cave
where Walter Scott, that tawdry Ulysses,
purloined a suffocated clansman's skull.
Crowns of Scottish kings were sacred; the lave
can whistle for dignity – who misses
them, peasants, slaves? Greeks, too, could shrug the cull.

Matt McGinn

We cannot see it, it keeps changing so.
All round us, *in and out, above, below,*
at evening, *phantom figures come and go,*
silently, *just a magic shadow show.*
A hoarse voice singing *come love watch with me*
was all we heard on that fog-shrouded bank.
We thought we saw him, but if so, he sank
into the irrecoverable sea.
Dear merry man, what is your country now?
Does it keep changing? Will we ever see it?
A crane, a backcourt, an accordion?
Or sherbet dabs, henna, and jasmined brow?
The book is clasped, and time will never free it.
Mektub. The caravan winds jangling on.

Post-Referendum

'No no, it will not do, it will not be.
I tell you you must leave your land alone.
Who do you think is poised to ring the phone?
Fish your straitjacket packet from the sea
you threw it in, get your headphones mended.
You don't want the world now, do you? Come on,
you're pegged out on your heathery futon,
take the matches from your lids, it's ended.'
We watched the strong sick dirkless Angel groan,
shiver, half-rise, batter with a shrunk wing
the space the Tempter was no longer in.
He tried to hear feet, calls, car-doors, shouts, drone
of engines, hooters, hear a meeting sing.
A coin clattered at the end of its spin.

Gangs

Naw naw, there's nae big wurds here, there ye go.
Christ man ye're in a bad wey, kin ye staun?
See here noo, wance we know jist where we're gaun,
we'll jump thon auld – stoap that, will ye – *Quango*.
Thaim that squealt *Lower Inflation*, aye, thaim,
plus thae *YY Zero Wage Increase* wans,
they'll no know what hit thim. See yours, and Dan's,
and mine's, that's three chibs. We'll soon hiv a team.
Whit's that? *Non-Index-Linked!* Did ye hear it?
Look! *Tiny Global Recession!* C'moan then,
ya bams, Ah'll take ye. *Market Power fae Drum!*
Dave, man, get up. Dave! Ach, ye're no near it.
Ah'm oan ma tod. But they'll no take a len
a me, Ah'm no deid yet, or deif, or dumb!

After a Death

A writer needs nothing but a table.
His pencil races, pauses, crosses out.
Five years ago he lost his friend, without
him he struggles through a different fable.
The one who died, he is the better one.
The other one is selfish, ruthless, he
uses people, floats in an obscure sea
of passions, half-drowns as the livid sun
goes down, calls out for help he will not give.
Examine yourself! He is afraid to.
But that is not quite true, I saw him look
into that terrible place, let him live
at least with what is eternally due
to love that lies in earth in cold Carluke.

The Buenos Aires Vase, one mile across,
flickering with unsleeping silent flames,
its marble carved in vine-leaves mixed with names,
shirtless ones and *desaparecidos*;
a collier's iron collar, riveted,
stamped by his Burntisland owner; a spade
from Babiy Yar; a blood-crust from the blade
that jumped the corpse of Wallace for his head;
the stout rack soaked in Machiavelli's sweat;
a fire-circled scorpion; a blown frog;
the siege of Beirut in stained glass; a sift
of Auschwitz ash; an old tapestry-set
unfinished, with a crowd, a witch, a log;
a lachrymatory no man can lift.

1983

'A parrot Edward Lear drew has just died.'
There was a young lady of Corstorphine
who adopted a psittacine orphan.
It shrieked and it cried: they threw far and wide
her ashes right over Corstorphine. Zoos
guard and pamper the abandoned squawkers,
tickle stories from the raunchy talkers,
shoulder a bold centenarian muse
over artists deaf as earth. 'Oho! Lear
sketched me, delirious old man, how he
shuffled about, his tabby on the sill,
a stew on the stove, a brush in his ear,
and sometimes hummed, or he buzzed like a bee,
painting parrots and all bright brave things still!'

A Place of Many Waters

Infinitely variable water,
let seals bob in your silk or loll on Mull
where the lazy fringes rustle; let hull
and screw slew you round, blind heavy daughter
feeling for shores; keep kelpies in loch lairs,
eels gliding, malts mashing, salmon springing;
let the bullers roar to the terns winging
in from a North Sea's German Ocean airs
of pressing crashing Prussian evening blue;
give linns long fall; bubble divers bravely
down to mend the cable you love to rust;
and slant at night through lamplit cities, true
as change is true, on gap-site pools, gravely
splintering the puckering of the gust.

The Poet in the City

Rain stockaded Glasgow; we paused, changed gears,
found him solitary but cheerful in
Anniesland, with the cheerfulness you'd win,
we imagined, through schiltrons of banked fears.
The spears had a most sombre glint, as if
the forced ranks had re-closed, but there he wrote
steadily, with a peg for the wet coat
he'd dry and put on soon. Gulls cut the cliff
of those houses, we watched him follow them
intently, see them beat and hear them scream
about the invisible sea they smelt
and fish-white boats they raked from stern to stem
although their freedom was in fact his dream
of freedom with all guilts all fears unfelt.

The Norn (1)

It was high summer, and the sun was hot.
We flew up over Perthshire, following
Christo's great-granddaughter in her swing-wing
converted crop-sprayer till plastic shot
above Schiehallion from her spinneret
Scotland-shaped and Scotland-sized, descended
silent, tough, translucent, light-attended,
catching that shoal of contours in one net.
Beneath it, what amazement; anger; some
stretching in wonder at a sky to touch;
chaos at airports, stunned larks, no more rain!
It would not burn, it would not cut. The hum
of civic protest probed like Dali's crutch.
Children ran wild under that counterpane.

The Norn (2)

But was it art? We asked the French, who said
La nature est un temple où les vivants
sont les piliers, which was at least not wrong
but did it answer us? Old Christo's head
rolled from its box, wrapped in rough manila.
'The pillars of the temple are the dead,'
it said, 'packed up and bonded into lead.'
Jowls of hemp smelt sweet like crushed vanilla.
But his descendant in her flying-suit
carefully put the head back in its place.
'Of course it's art,' she said, 'we just use men.
Pygmalion got it inside out, poor brute.
For all they've been made art, they've not lost face.
They'll lift the polythene, be men again.'

The Target

Then they were running with fire in their hair,
men and women were running everywhere,
women and children burning everywhere,
ovens of death were falling from the air.
Lucky seemed those at the heart of the blast
who left no flesh or ash or blood or bone,
only a shadow on dead Glasgow's stone,
when the black angel had gestured and passed.
Rhu was a demon's pit, Faslane a grave;
the shattered basking sharks that thrashed Loch Fyne
were their killer's tocsin: 'Where I am, watch;
when I raise one arm to destroy, I save
none; increase, multiply; vengeance is mine;
in no universe will man find his match.'

After Fallout

A giant gannet buzzed our glinty probe.
Its forty-metre wing-span hid the sun.
Life was stirring, the fallout time was done.
From *a stick-nest in Ygdrasil* the globe
was hatching genes like rajahs' koh-i-noors.
Over St Kilda, house-high poppy-beds
made forests; towering sea-pinks turned the heads
of even master mariners with lures
that changed the white sea-graves to scent-drenched groves.
Fortunate Isles! The gannet bucked our ship
with a quick sidelong swoop, clapped its wings tight,
dived, and exploding through the herring droves
dragged up a flailing manta by the lip
and flew it, twisting slowly, out of sight.

The Age of Heracleum

The jungle of Gleneagles was a long
shadow on our right as we travelled down.
Boars rummaged through the ballroom's toppled crown
of chandeliers and mashed the juicy throng
of giant hogweed stalks. Wild tramps with sticks
glared, kept a rough life. South in Fife we saw
the rusty buckled bridges, the firth raw
with filth and flower-heads, dead fish, dark slicks.
We stood in what had once been Princes Street.
Hogweed roots thrust, throbbed underneath for miles.
The rubble of the shops became the food
of new cracks running mazes round our feet,
and west winds blew, past shattered bricks and tiles,
millions of seeds through ruined Holyrood.

Computer Error: Neutron Strike

No one was left to hear the long All Clear.
Hot wind swept through the streets of Aberdeen
and stirred the corpse-clogged harbour. Each machine,
each building, tank, car, college, crane, stood sheer
and clean but that a shred of skin, a hand,
a blackened child driven like tumbleweed
would give the lack of ruins leave to feed
on horrors we were slow to understand
but did. Boiling fish-floating seas slopped round
the unmanned rigs that flared into the night;
the videos ran on, sham death, sham love;
the air-conditioners kept steady sound.
An automatic foghorn, and its light
warned out to none below, and none above.

Inward Bound

Flapping, fluttering, like imploding porridge
being slowly uncooked on anti-gas,
the Grampians were a puny shrinking mass
of cairns and ski-tows sucked back to their orig-
ins. Pylons rumbled downwards; lighthouses
hissed into bays; reactors popped, ate earth.
We watched a fissure struggling with the girth
of old Glamis, but down it went. Boots, blouses,
hats, hands above heads, like feet-first divers
all those inhabitants pressed in to meet
badgers and stalactites, and to build in reverse
tenements deepest for late arrivers,
and domes to swim in, not to echo feet
or glow down, dim, on the draped, chanted hearse.

The Desert

There was a time when everything was sand.
It drifted down from Findhorn, south south south
and sifted into eye and ear and mouth
on battlefield or bed or plough-bent land.
Loose wars grew sluggish, and the bugles choked.
We saw some live in caves, and even tombs.
Mirages rose from dry Strathspey in plumes.
Scorpions appeared. Heaven's fires were stoked.
But soon they banded to bind dunes in grass,
made cactus farms, ate lizards, sank their wells.
They had their rough strong songs, rougher belief.
Did time preserve them through that narrow pass?
Or are they Guanches under conquerors' spells,
chiselled on sorry plinths in Tenerife?

The Coin

We brushed the dirt off, held it to the light.
The obverse showed us *Scotland*, and the head
of a red deer; the antler-glint had fled
but the fine cut could still be felt. All right:
we turned it over, read easily *One Pound*,
but then the shock of Latin, like a gloss,
Respublica Scotorum, sent across
such ages as we guessed but never found
at the worn edge where once the date had been
and where as many fingers had gripped hard
as hopes their silent race had lost or gained.
The marshy scurf crept up to our machine,
sucked at our boots. Yet nothing seemed ill-starred.
And least of all the realm the coin contained.

The Solway Canal

Slowly through the Cheviot Hills at dawn
we sailed. The high steel bridge at Carter Bar
passed over us in fog with not a car
in its broad lanes. Our hydrofoil slid on,
vibrating quietly through wet rock walls
and scarves of dim half-sparkling April mist;
a wizard with a falcon on his wrist
was stencilled on our bow. Rough waterfalls
flashed on that northern island of the Scots
as the sun steadily came up and cast
red light along the uplands and the waves,
and gulls with open beaks tore out our thoughts
through the thick glass to where the Eildons massed,
or down to the Canal's drowned borderers' graves.

A Scottish Japanese Print

Lighter and lighter, not eternity,
only a morning breaking on dark fields.
The sleepers might almost throw back those shields,
jump to stations as if golden pity
could probe the grave, the beauty was so great
in that silent slowly brightening place.
No, it is the living who wait for grace,
the hare, the fox, the farmer at the gate.
And Glasgow's windows took the strong spring sun
in the corner of a water-meadow,
its towers shadowed by a pigeon's flight.
Not daisy-high, children began to run
like tumbling jewels, as in old Yeddo,
and with round eyes unwound their wild red kit.

Outward Bound

– That was the time Scotland began to move.
– Scotland move? No, it is impossible!
– It became an island, and was able
to float in the Atlantic lake and prove
crannogs no fable. Like a sea-washed log
it loved to tempt earnest geographers,
duck down and dub them drunk hydrographers,
shake itself dry, no longer log but dog.
– Was it powered? On stilts? – Amazing grace
was found in granite, it moved on pure sound.
Greenland twisted round to hear it, Key West
whistled, waved, Lanzarote's ashy face
cracked open with laughter. There was no ground
of being, only being, sweetest and best.

On Jupiter

Scotland was found on Jupiter. That's true.
We lost all track of time, but there it was.
No one told us its origins, its cause.
A simulacrum, a dissolving view?
It seemed as solid as a terrier
shaking itself dry from a brisk black swim
in the reservoir of Jupiter's grim
crimson trustless eye. No soul-ferrier
guarded the swampy waves. Any gods there,
if they had made the thing in play, were gone,
and if the land had launched its own life out
among the echoes of inhuman air,
its launchers were asleep, or had withdrawn,
throwing their stick into a sea of doubt.

Clydegrad

It was so fine we lingered there for hours.
The long broad streets shone strongly after rain.
Sunset blinded the tremble of the crane
we watched from, dazed the heliport-towers.
The mile-high buildings flashed, flushed, greyed, went dark,
greyed, flushed, flashed, chameleons under flak
of cloud and sun. The last far thunder-sack
ripped and spilled its grumble. Ziggurat-stark,
a power-house reflected in the lead
of the old twilight river leapt alive
lit up at every window, and a boat
of students rowed past, slid from black to red
into the blaze. But where will they arrive
with all, boat, city, earth, like them, afloat?

A Golden Age

That must have been a time of happiness.
The air was mild, the Campsie Fells had vines.
Dirigible parties left soft sky-signs
and bursts of fading music. Who could guess
what they might not accomplish, they had seas
in cities, cities in the sea; their domes
and crowded belvederes hung free, their homes
eagle-high or down among whitewashed quays.
And women sauntered often with linked arms
through night streets, or alone, or danced a maze
with friends. Perhaps it did not last. What lasts?
The bougainvillea millenniums
may come and go, but then in thistle days
a strengthened seed outlives the hardest blasts.

The Summons

The year was ending, and the land lay still.
Despite our countdown, we were loath to go,
kept padding along the ridge, the broad glow
of the city beneath us, and the hill
swirling with a little mist. Stars were right,
plans, power; only now this unforeseen
reluctance, like a slate we could not clean
of characters, yet could not read, or write
our answers on, or smash, or take with us.
Not a hedgehog stirred. We sighed, climbed in, locked.
If it was love we felt, would it not keep,
and travel where we travelled? Without fuss
we lifted off, but as we checked and talked
a far horn grew to break that people's sleep.

Eleven struck. The traffic lights were green.
The shuddering machine let out its roar
As we sprang forward into brilliant streets.
Beyond your shoulders and helmet the walls rose
Well into darkness, mounted up, plunged past –
Hunting the clouds that hunted the few stars.
And now the neons thinned, the moon was huge.
The gloomy river lay in a glory, the bridge
In its mists as we rode over it slowly sighed.
We lost the shining tram-lines in the slums
As we kept south; the shining trolley-wires
Glinted through Gorbals; on your helmet a glint hung.
A cat in a crumbling close-mouth, a lighted window
With its shadow-play, a newspaper in the wind –
The night swept them up even as we slowed,
Our wheels jolting over the buckled causeys.
But my net swept up night and cat and road
And mine is the shadow-play that window showed
And mine the paper with its cries and creases.
– Shadow-play? What we flashed past was life
As what we flash into is life, and life
Will not stand still until within one flash
Of words or paint or human love it stops
Transfixed, and drops its pain and grime
Into forgetful time.
But I remember: I saw the flash: and then
We met the moonlit Clyde again, swung off
And roared in a straight run for Rutherglen.
The wind whistled by the football ground

And by the waste ground that the seagulls found.
The long wail of a train recalled the city
We had left behind, and mingled with the wind.
Whatever it was that sang in me there
As we neared home, I give it no name here.
But tenements and lives, the wind, our wheels,
The vibrant windshield and your guiding hands
Fell into meaning, whatever meaning it was –
Whatever joy it was –
And my blood quickened in me as I saw
Everything guided, vibrant, where our shadow
Glided along the pavements and the walls.
Perhaps I only saw the thoroughfares,
The river, the dancing of the foundry-flares?
Joy is where long solitude dissolves.
I rode with you towards human needs and cares.

1956

25

If you ask what my favourite programme is
it has to be that strange world jigsaw final.
After the winner had defeated all his rivals
with harder and harder jigsaws, he had to prove his mettle
by completing one last absolute mindcrusher
on his own, under the cameras, in less than a week.
We saw, but he did not, what the picture would be:
the mid-Atlantic, photographed from a plane,
as featureless a stretch as could be found,
no weeds, no flotsam, no birds, no oil, no ships,
the surface neither stormy nor calm, but ordinary,
a light wind on a slowly rolling swell.
Hand-cut by a fiendish jigger to simulate,
but not to have, identical beaks and bays,
it seemed impossible; but the candidate –
he said he was a stateless person, called himself Smith –
was impressive: small, dark, nimble, self-contained.
The thousands of little grey tortoises were scattered
on the floor of the studio; we saw the clock; he started.
His food was brought to him, but he hardly ate.
He had a bed, with the light only dimmed to a weird blue,
never out. By the first day he had established
the edges, saw the picture was three metres long
and appeared to represent (dear God!) the sea.
Well, it was a man's life, and the silence
(broken only by sighs, click of wood, plop of coffee
in paper cups) that kept me fascinated.
Even when one hand was picking the edge-pieces
I noticed his other hand was massing sets
of distinguishing ripples or darker cross-hatching or
incipient wave-crests; his mind,

if not his face, worked like a sea.
It was when he suddenly rose from his bed
at two, on the third night, went straight over
to one piece and slotted it into a growing central patch,
then back to bed, that I knew he would make it.
On the sixth day he looked haggard and slow,
with perhaps a hundred pieces left,
of the most dreary unmarked lifeless grey.
The camera showed the clock more frequently.
He roused himself, and in a quickening burst
of activity, with many false starts, began
to press that inhuman insolent remnant together.
He did it, on the evening of the sixth day.
People streamed onto the set. Bands played.
That was fine. But what I liked best
was the last shot of the completed sea,
filling the screen; then the saw-lines disappeared,
till almost imperceptibly the surface moved
and it was again the real Atlantic, glad
to distraction to be released, raised
above itself in growing gusts, allowed
to roar as rain drove down and darkened,
allowed to blot, for a moment, the orderer's hand.

26

What was the best programme?
Oh, it was Giotto's O.
I don't argue the case
that it really was the past,
tapped under conditions
made suddenly favourable.
But how could any actor

so unpreparedly, so
swiftly yet so surely and
so gloriously seize
a sheet of pure white paper
and with a black loaded brush
paint a perfect circle?
The camera was so close
that no trick or device
could have stayed undetected.
No, it was Giotto's O.
The papal envoy, I observed,
crossed himself at the sight –
needlessly, there was no magic
either black or white, it
was only the life of a man
concentrated down
to his finger-tips in the great
final ease of creation
which in its silence and
no longer laboriously
circles round and out.

27

The programme that stays most in my mind
was one you called the Dance of the Letters.
The graphics here was altogether
crisp and bright and strong and real.
First that gallows, with the dust
whirling across the square to sting
a blackened and unfeeling face
and tear at the unreadable placard
pinned to its slowly twisting chest

resolved itself into a T.
Then the car, in bird's-eye view,
crawling through narrow streets to bang
its bomb-load and its girl martyr
into a crowded market-place
stopped, became a fiery H.
Mothers, children, grandfathers, all
knew how to line the desert dirt-road
in a few black rags, and stretch out bowls
in their twig arms or hold out only
arms, till their appeal froze
in stifling fly-black heat to form
an E. But then another E
was gently, tentatively drawn
from the hard, half-shining prongs
of a rake; the gnarled gardener
was keeping his patch clean and rich,
weedless and airy, able to deliver
the vegetables of the year.
In a courtyard, shaded with awnings,
where a tethered, slew-mouthed camel chewed,
one red earthen water-jar
as old as history waited in its stand,
turning at last into an N.
A fisherwoman, pregnant, walked
slowly along a rocky shore,
but then transformed into a ship
with blowing spinnaker sailed out
in her whole woman's life to break
silence only with the whipping
of the sheets and with the song
she or the wind threw back to us.
She left us, melted into the white
of a D that rang out through the blue.

THE DOWSER

With my forked branch of Lebanese cedar
I quarter the dunes like downs and guide
an invisible plough far over the sand.
But how to quarter such shifting acres
when the wind melts their shapes, and shadows
mass where all was bright before,
and landmarks walk like wraiths at noon?
All I know is that underneath,
how many miles no one can say,
an unbroken water-table waits
like a lake; it has seen no bird or sail
in its long darkness, and no man;
not even pharaohs dug so far
for all their thirst, or thirst of glory,
or thrust-power of ten thousand slaves.
I tell you I can smell it though,
that water. I am old and black
and I know the manners of the sun
which makes me bend, not break. I lose
my ghostly footprints without complaint.
I put every mirage in its place.
I watch the lizard make its lace.
Like one not quite blind I go
feeling for the sunken face.
So hot the days, the nights so cold,
I gather my white rags and sigh
but sighing step so steadily
that any vibrance in so deep
a lake would never fail to rise
towards the snowy cedar's bait.
Great desert, let your sweetness wake.

Dear man, my love goes out in waves
and breaks. Whatever is, craves.
Terrible the cage
to see all life from, brilliantly about,
crowds, pavements, cars, or hear the common shout
of goals in a near park.
But now the black bars arc
blue in my breath – split – part –
I'm out – it's art,
it's love, it's rage –

Standing in rage in decent air
will never clear the place of care.
Simply to be
should be enough, in the same city, and let
absurd despair tramp and roar off-set.
Be satisfied with it,
the gravel and the grit
the struggling eye can't lift,
the veils that drift,
the weird to dree.

Press close to me at midnight as
you say goodbye; that's what it has
to offer, life
I mean. Into the frost with you; into
the bed with me; and get the light out too.
Better to shake unseen
and let real darkness screen
the shadows of the heart,
the vacant part-
ner, husband, wife.

Acclaim was one of eighty thousand waving and bristling in the stadium; his ears crackled in the squeezing heat as he moved with the surge.

Celt was a harp of cobwebs; when they plucked him in the morning he yielded creaks and shivers, a scrape of pure mildew.

Corgi grew up on aircraft steps but never rooted well; his dwarfish habit came from too much handling.

Delta was seldom tracked down; she ran like quicksilver through the monsoons and left an India of children thrusting spears at the sun.

Doublet was woven tight and velvety and pulsed like a heart; they cut him down with pikes.

Flare came suddenly, like a moor-burn, a royal flush, a tenth wave, wild airs and rounded clouds jostled to solicit him.

Golden Promise shook his spiky hair and straddled the shore; cows' tongues rasped his belly when he turned white with salt.

Gold Marker strode over the hill's flank unfurling his strawy banner next to the hot yellow patch of rape; he whistled, and marched like mustard.

Golf had a rough time but grew stoic and hardy; prone on the headland he pricked his ears like flags.

Javelin struck hard and straight through the rain and shone; gloved harvesters swore as the steely beards drew blood and clanked down the chute for robots' bannocks.

Klaxon was so strong he made rutting stags stumble; brewed Thor's mash in Asgard.

Kym leaned lightly, listening; too far off her father Kandym stalked the wastelands, binding and rebinding the restless Kara Kum from his bag of marram.

Lina crouched in a tangled sea of tresses at the feet of Jesus; her roots moaned for the crop they had still to give.

Midas swaggered in a cave-mouth, lolled on couch-grass, played with bear-bones; now gapes, purple, staring, drowned in his seed-hoard.

Nairn was agoraphobic, itched to be malted, doze ten years in casks; a second life under ribs of men.

Natasha bent down her drear dark brows as the thousand-mile-old wind swept to her across the steppe; unbreaking bent down, bowed down, bore unbroken.

Piccolo piped the high meadows awake; his pink-shears gave the dawn chorus an edge.

Themis swayed to the left, to the right, courtly, with all her companions; a chorus of measure, the breathing of the earth, in a windless field.

Vista was a blue-eyed tundra-watcher, hard as nails; when the Yenisei came roaring through her bed she snapped her fingers and cast grain in his face, extending her empire north, towards the ice.

MAKING A POEM

Coming in with it
from frost and buses
gently burning
you must prepare it
with luck
to go critical.
Give the hook your scarf,
the chrome hook, maybe,
your green scarf. Say
Smoky Smoky
to the cat, set him
on his cushion, perhaps
a patch cushion
from old Perth.
Put the kettle on,
go to the window,
mist the glass
dreaming a minute lightly,
boys on the ice,
rows of orange lamps.
And go cut
white new bread.
Make tea like skaters' leaves.
You're never free.
It's blue dark night again.
Below the panes
in quietness.
Take a pencil
like the milkman's horse
round and round.

But you must agree
with it, and love it,
even when it grows
too fierce for favour.
It comes, and the cat shines.
And make the poem now.

1968

BY THE FIRE

That night I was your father and mother, I broke
your solitude, I cradled something that you became.
You cried my name.
How wildly we had turned! I smoothed
your brow where we lay in the glow,
kissed you so deep, so long, it was
as if I had moved a key
in the door of desolation,
you were almost weeping
thinking of your dead brother the apple of your eye
crushed in that torn car-metal, your dead sister
grotesque on the black ice, your mother in her grave –
your years of waiting, half life, half death –
your diffidence, your fear –
but I was then your brother and your sister, in
the dance of the fire with your head in my arms.

I will take all the black ice of Lanarkshire
from the heart that only needs love.
What I give you, give me,
and break me free.

1963

TRILOBITES

A grey-blue slab, fanned like a pigeon's wing,
stands on my record cabinet
between a lamp and a speaker.
Trapped in a sea of solid stone
the trilobites still almost swim;
the darker grey of their backs,
thumbnail-sized and thumbnail-shaped,
gives out a dull shine as I switch on the lamp.
I have eight of them; half are crushed, but
two are almost perfect, lacking nothing but the antennas.
My fingertip, coarse and loutish
tracing the three delicate rows of furrowed plates,
tries to read that paleozoic braille
as vainly as the blast of Wagner at their ear
searches for entrance five hundred million years
and a world of air too late. But I would not trade
my family torn by chance from time
for Grecian urn or gold Byzantium.

BLACKBIRD MARIGOLDS

It's morning
with five marigolds
in a dewy tumbler
the sun shines through
as I hold it high
from the long grasses

– You can't come in
I'm not –
– Oh yes I can

with my wet marigolds
dripping on the floor
and stand behind you
fold you round
to smell the faint
fresh cut gold
petals –
my head in your hair
the window open
the door open
coffee on the stove
the garden all
one song of blackbirds

1970

SEVEN DECADES

At ten I read Mayakovsky had died,
learned my first word of Russian, *lyublyu*,
watched my English teacher poke his earwax
with a well-chewed HB and get the class
to join his easy mocking of my essay
where I'd used *verdant herbage* for *green grass*.
So he was right? So I hated him!
And he was not really right, the ass.
A writer knows what he needs,
as came to pass.

At twenty I got marching orders, kitbag,
farewell to love, not arms (though our sole arms
were stretchers), a freezing Glentress winter

where I was coaxing sticks at six to get
a stove hot for the cooks, found myself picked
quartermaster's clerk – 'this one seems a bit
less gormless than the bloody others' – did
gas drill in the stinging tent, met
Tam McSherry who farted at will
a musical set.

At thirty I thought life had passed me by,
translated *Beowulf* for want of love.
And one night stands in city centre lanes –
they were dark in those days – were wild but bleak.
Sydney Graham in London said 'you know
I always thought so', kissed me on the cheek.
And I translated Rilke's *Loneliness*
is like a rain, and week after week after week
strained to unbind myself,
sweated to speak.

At forty I woke up, saw it was day,
found there was love, heard a new beat, heard Beats,
sent airmail solidarity to São
Paulo's poetic-concrete revolution,
knew Glasgow – what? – knew Glasgow new – somehow –
new with me, with John, with cranes, diffusion
of another concrete revolution, not bad,
not good, but new. And new was no illusion:
a spring of words, a sloughing,
an ablution.

At fifty I began to have bad dreams
of Palestine, and saw bad things to come,
began to write my long unwritten war.
I was a hundred-handed Sindbad then,
rolled and unrolled carpets of blood and love,
raised tents of pain, made the dust into men
and laid the dust with men. I supervised
a thesis on Doughty, that great Englishman
who brought all Arabia back
in his hard pen.

At sixty I was standing by a grave.
The winds of Lanarkshire were loud and high.
I knew what I had lost, what I had had.
The East had schooled me about fate, but still
it was the hardest time, oh more, it was
the worst of times in self-reproach, the will
that failed to act, the mass of good not done.
Forgiveness must be like the springs that fill
deserted furrows if they wait
until – until –

At seventy I thought I had come through,
like parting a bead curtain in Port Said,
to something that was shadowy before,
figures and voices of late times that might
be surprising yet. The beads clash faintly
behind me as I go forward. No candle-light
please, keep that for Europe. Switch the whole thing
right on. When I go in I want it bright,
I want to catch whatever is there
in full sight.

PERSUASION

You never thought much of the darkness, did you?
You wanted everything so open, open –
I said it could not be – you laughed, and shook me,
and pointed me and swivelled me to windows,
doors, rivers, skies – said it must be, must issue
right out if it was to have any honour –
what: love? – yes: love; it must seal up its burrow,
must take a stair or two, a flight or two, for
poles, horizons, convoys, elevations –
but tender still to backcourts and dim woodlands.
Oh, never ask where darkness is if light can
break down the very splinters of the jambs – be
sure I know you can take in the sunlight
through every pore and nothing will be blinded
or shrivelled up like moth in flame or crippled
by some excess of nakedness – just give it,
your intelligence, your faith I really mean, your
faith, that's it, to see the streets so brilliant
after gales you really can go out there,
you really can have something of that gladness,
many things under the sun, and not disheartened,
so many in their ways going beside you.

AN ABANDONED CULVERT

The daffodils sang shrill within the culvert.
Their almost acid notes amazed the darkness
culverts are happiest with. They could not cower,
the yellow birds, pure cries on stilts, conundrums
to burst the reason of those mineral courses.
Five stubborn half-fluted half-ragged non-fluting trumpets

blared the dank brickfall grit into submission.
Whatever daffodils can say, they said it
louder and sharper than the stalagmites they
might have been, if all the timorous ages
had managed to conspire against some thrusting
of the dumb seed that could not know, yet knew, it
had to unapologetically
proclaim a yellow and not golden treasure
unyielding to the kisses of the digger.

A CITY

– What was all that then? – What? – *That*. That was *Glasgow*.
It's a film, an epic, lasts for, anyway
keep watching, it's not real, so everything is
melting at the edges and could go, you have to
remember some of it was shot in Moscow,
parts in Chicago, and then of course the people
break up occasionally, they're only graphics,
look there's two businessmen gone zigzag, they'll be
off-screen in one moment, yes, I thought so.
– What a sky though. – Ah well, the sky is listed,
change as it may. It's a peculiar platinum
with roary sunset flecks and fissures, rigging
was best against it, gone now, don't regret it,
move on, and if you wait you'll see some children,
oh it's a fine effect, maybe they're real, some
giant children pulling down a curtain
of platinum and scarlet stuff as airy
as it seems strong, and they'll begin to play there,
bouncing their shrill cries till it's too dark to
catch a shadow running along the backcloth,

and they still won't go home, despite the credits.
– You mean the film goes on, beyond the credits?
– You'll have to wait and see, won't you? It's worth it.
– I'm not persuaded even of its existence.
– What, *Glasgow?* – The city, not the film. – The city
is the film. – Oh come on. – I tell you. – Right then,
look. Renfield Street, marchers, banners, slogans.
Read the message, hear the chant. – Lights! Camera!
– But where are the children? – That I grant you;
somewhere, huge presences; shouting, laughter;
hunch-cuddy-hunch against a phantom housewall.

IL TRAVIATO

That's my eyes at their brightest and biggest.
It's belladonna. I've a friend who. Not that
I'd ever use too much, did once, came out of
delirium after a week of sweats, you learn. But
I'm so pale now, some men like the contrast
as I stand in the park with my eyes burning,
or glide among the poplars, they're thin as I am
but seem to manage, get their light, get nourished
as I get trade although the Wraith's my nickname.
I ought to be in bed, probably, maybe.
In any case my lover sends me out now,
he says it's all I'm good for, bring some money.
He hides my razor till I'm 'interesting',
a chalky portrait ruffed in my black stubble.
I mustn't be too hard on him. The years we.
It all comes down to what kind of constant
you believe in, doesn't it, not mathematics
but as if you had the faintest brilliance

that was only yours, not to let any sickness
douse it, or despair creeping with a snuffer.
I sometimes think I wish it could be ended
– those hard-faced brutes that hit you at the climax –
but then I go on, don't I, as everyone
should, pressing through the streets with glances
for all and everything, not to miss crumbs of
life, drops of the crowded flowing wonder.

A VANGUARD

We came to the end of the world at midnight.
Someone called out from the back of the column,
Is that it then? What is it like? I answered,
Whatever you have of imagination
you must use. Come forward. All of you. Stand easy.
Through so much dust, we were no smart company,
but somehow the tired group seemed monumental
as any old stone circle where they clustered
gravely over staves and rifles and brooded
above the yelling abyss we'd reached the lip of.
And those who thought a globe could never have one –
abyss, I mean, edge, rim, sick slope to vacancy –
began to shiver at celestial mechanics
crumbling away. It must be a ravine then,
fog, darkness, the farther bank is hidden –
one of them said, using imagination.
No one believed that rational man; the spirit
of the place, our chilling sweat, the terrible groaning
from throats unseen below our feet, took toll of
any reason we had left. What had we looked for
in fact but the end of the world, we the vanguard

sent out to scotch or seal appalling rumours.
So there we were. Was it hell? We saw no one.
The cold grew more intense. Let's go back then,
I said, it's not the end of the world. Joking
broke the spell. Someone laughed. A ravine surely,
windy caves and flues like voices. And supper
a short march away. Soon they would start whistling.
I kept my thoughts, but nothing would do, nothing.
No end in time was near, or in space possible.
As for the dead, who am I to appease them,
a scout, a ragged man, a storyteller?

AUNT MYRA (1901–1989)

A horse in a field in a picture is easy.
A man in a room with a fan, we wonder.
It might be whirring blades in steamy downtown –
but no, it's what she's left beside her dance-cards.
How she sat out a foxtrot at the Plaza
and fanned her brow, those far-off flirty Twenties
he opens and shuts with an unpractised gesture
that leaves the years half-laughing at the pathos
of the clumsy, until rising strings have swept them
dancing again into silence. The room darkens
with a blue lingering glow above the roof-tops
but the man still stands there, holding up the dangling
dance-cards by their tiny attached pencils.
The cords which are so light seem to him heavy
as if they were about to take the strain of
tender evenings descending into memory.
Something is hard, not easy, though it's clearly
a man, a fan, a woman, a room, a picture.

URBAN GUNFIRE

'Civilians' are not really, truly, people.
As regimes fall, they're only 'caught in crossfire'.
Expendablest of the expendable, they
crawl, or if they're lucky someone drags them,
to doorways where they slump and shake till nightfall.
How great it must be not to be civilian
or anything but gun in hand, young, mobile,
slogan-fuelled better than machines are,
you cannot even hear the shattered housewife,
far less see her blood and bags and bread, it's
bullet time between you and your sniper,
hot streaks go shopping, nothing else goes shopping,
no one is out there in the open, we are,
we are it and it is where they vanish
like a clapped piece of tawdry human magic,
too feeble to be seen by psyched-up fighters.
Their cries are in another world. The trigger
is steady as they roll about the tarmac.
And it goes on as if it could not finish.

A FUCHSIA

I rescued it three years ago from rubbish.
Half-dead, a limp ungainly arc of ripped-off
green, it lay without a flower to recommend it
and somehow like a spring or snake it challenged
the logic of the vertical, resisted
potting; but I firmed it, staked it, waited.
Sometimes it's barish, sometimes bushy; tries, though.
This summer it decided to be bushy,
parachutes pushed out, dangling pink and purple,

trembling as container lorries rumbled,
almost nodding to make me say I loved them,
and so I do, you hear that, you strange plant you,
it's true. You don't love me but I sense something –
no I can't be mistake, it's next to palpable –
you're bent, a down-turned cup-hook, and without propping
you would collapse into the earth you came from,
so why should you keep flowering so gamely –
I can't but think it speaks to me, your living
loaded curve of grace steadily bearing,
but the best bearing, the best blooming, is moral,
or if that cannot be – who am I to say so,
is chlorophyll so dumb – at least I'm sending,
like an antenna – don't shake, I don't mean insects –
waves of encouragement, solidarities of
struggle, gratitude even for imaginary
gratitude, though who knows what a fuschia
feels, plucked from dump and dust, from a gehenna
to this west kitchen window, rays of evening
and more mysterious light of human glances.

A FLYPAST

Symphonic shreds had just swept off with Schnittke
when two swans flew like spirits past my window.
Russia, music, soul, said the television,
nature, it said, harmony, ideal.
The long necks stretched, smelt their swan lake, laboured
forward till the trees hid them. And eastern,
the television said, Armenian, Azeri
horizontality, the patterns endless,
keeping western verticals at bay while

voices circle over silent marshes.
Well, I don't know. My startling flyers flapping
so steady and so low over the van-tops,
the hissing wheels, the sirens and the skateboards,
knew where they were going and had shattered
in their rising from some placid water mirror
a harmony too famous, strode the air-streams
to turn how many heads at windows as we
wonder that we ever thought them spirits,
those muscles working, those webs, that eye, that purpose.

FIRES

What is that place, my father and my mother,
you have gone to, I think of, in the ashes
of the air and not the earth, better to go there
than under stones or in any remembrance
but mine and that of others who once loved you,
fewer year on year. It is midsummer
and till my voice broke, *Summer suns are glowing*
I loved to sing and *One fine day* to hear from
some thin wild old gramophone that carried
its passion across the Rutherglen street, invisibly
played again and again – I thought of that person,
him or her, as taking me to a country
far high sunny where I knew to be happy
was only a moment, a puttering flame in the fireplace
but burning all the misery to cinders
if it could, a sift of dross like what we mourn for
as caskets sinks with horrifying blandness
into a roar, into smoke, into light, into almost nothing.
The not quite nothing I praise it and I write it.

A MANIFESTO

The futurists took ties to yellow parties.
The futurists thought life a bobby-dazzler.
The futurists made heady love to airships.
The futurists made heavy words go heady.
The futurists got canvas off its hindlegs.
The futurists threw music off its shirtfront.
The futurists gesamtkunstwerked the bolshies.
The futurists shot off montage's visa.
The futurists flew kites up up up endless.
The futurists kept dynamos in kennels.
The futurists had soaring paper cities.
The futurists lie snoring in real cities.
The futurists are dreaming of red pigeons.
The futurists hold hands among the atoms.
The futurists, united, shall never be defeated.
The futurists, united, shall never be defeated.

LAMPS

And if anyone should tell our adventures,
remember that the universe has spaces
as well as forms – abysses, deserts, niches,
distances without even time as pedlar
to bring you, if you waited, explanations.
No, we have seen what we have seen, but often
there is a blank you must not fill with monsters.
It is all for what is to come after.
It is for the duguth of firm intent, the voyage
he and she and they must take, and you quiet
but trembling in your chair, rising, following
the light you catch, swinging but never vanishing,
into great deeps, our helmet-lamps, beckoning.

from BEASTS OF SCOTLAND

Wolf

Bring back the wolf!
He's not long gone, you know.
He went out when sheep came in.
Sheep cleared men and women.
Now let wolves clear sheep.
A little wildness please,
a little howling to be heard from the chalets,
a circling of yellow eyes at Aviemore.
That legend much discredited,
of the following of the sledges,
let us test it in the Cairngorms,
in the winter playgrounds with their merry cries,
in the white paths through the forest.
It would be good to get not a few scalps
to crawl with fear when they hear
that eerie arctic song
as one by one the muzzles
lift and open in the dark,
and the dark is long.

Midge

The evening is perfect, my sisters.
The loch lies silent, the air is still.
The sun's last rays linger over the water
and there is a faint smirr, almost a smudge
of summer rain. Sisters, I smell supper,
and what is more perfect than supper?
It is emerging from the wood,
in twos and threes, a dozen in all,

making such a chatter and a clatter
as it reaches the rocky shore,
admiring the arrangements of the light.
See the innocents, my sisters,
the clumsy ones, the laughing ones,
the rolled-up sleeves and the flapping shorts,
there is even a kilt (god of the midges,
you are good to us!). So gather your forces,
leave your tree-trunks, forsake the rushes,
fly up from the sour brown mosses
to the sweet flesh of face and forearm.
Think of your eggs. What does the egg need?
Blood, and blood. Blood is what the egg needs.
Our men have done their bit, they've gone,
it was all they were good for, poor dears. Now
it is up to us. The egg is quietly screaming
for supper, blood, supper, blood, supper!
Attack, my little Draculas, my Amazons!
Look at those flailing arms and stamping feet.
They're running, swatting, swearing, oh they're hopeless.
Keep at them, ladies. This is a feast.
This is a midsummer night's dream.
Soon we shall all lie down filled and rich,
and lay, and lay, and lay, and lay, and lay.

Gannet

High the cliffs, and
blue the sky, and
mad the spray, and
bright the sun, and
deep as the grave
the teeming waters

never at rest
in St Kilda's cauldron.
Fish for the taking
lazing in innocence
island to island,
flesh for a thunderbolt
not thrown by dogs,
not a Greek, not a Gael.
If the fish could look up:
a bird left the crag
white against the blue,
half hovered, half circled,
stopped in an air-path
with eye unblinking,
folded its wings, and
gravity-batteried,
sharp beak down, and
sharp tail up, it
plunged, it
plummeted, it
hit the sea, it
shot right under, and
vanished except
to the fish it speared
in a fearful irruption
from a heaven unseen.
So who is safe?
The gannet cliffs
are shrieking, but
not about that.

Seal

– Mother, I can hear a baby crying,
Out there in the sea, is it drowning or dying?

– No no, my lamb, that's not what you hear.
It is only a seal, go to sleep, never fear.

– There's another, and another, oh it is so sad.
How can an animal make us feel bad?

– I don't know, my dear, maybe they smell
The fishermen with clubs, fearful and fell.

– Why do they kill them? No wonder they cry.
Do the men never have a tear in their eye?

– Oh no, the seals kill the beautiful fish
That make our supper a beautiful dish.

– And we kill the fish. Everything we kill.
We dig a grave and it's too big to fill!

– Darling, it has to be. We are killed too.
Seventy years and the message comes through.

– Oh mother, the night is so cold and so wild!
Listen, listen, I am sure it is a child!

Wildcat

When did you last see me?
Never, perhaps.
You saw the ferns moving – was it the wind?
It's true the fronds are a good camouflage
for my stripes, but I can tell you
I was not there, not then.
Does that make it any easier,
I mean, that you really failed to miss anything?
If you still want to meet
this shy, solitary, rare etcetera –
well do you? – one of those days
when I am not snatching rabbits
but casing your chicken-coop? –
not extinct, you know, maybe a spirit –
spirit of Scotland, eh? – I haven't lost
my drift: here you are then,
meeting me, at the wire of the hen-run,
twilight woods behind, I'm doing my crouching
and spitting, gently lashing a bushy tail,
all right? You want to communicate?
Try to stroke me, lose a finger.
Try to tame me, lose a face.
But frankly this is academic.
I shun farms, crofts, dogs, guns; I've had that.
Where I love to be, I doubt
if you will ever find me.
I prowl the high bracken.
I am comforted by the rocks.
I rub the harsh trunks
of the Caledonian forest,
a ghost among ghosts.

Salmon

We hung over the falls, watching.
The river groaned as the gorge narrowed,
its turmoil was white, extravagant.
All this was far below. Once through,
it was crashed on by the waterfall
in a sort of massed chaos. The splashes
were brilliant, the spray was very fine.
A rainbow dared to cross the uproar.
That was not what we came to see.
But there they were, one, two, six,
some red, hook-jawed, stacked and packed with
energies they brought from Greenland,
backs, snouts testing the spumy
half air half-water element
they must jump through, even fly through –
they sprang, they soared, they gaped, they gasped,
lashed frantic tails, fell back, quivered,
lurched up again, making it, some,
some stunned on rocks, but a great one
first, high, and his mate soon after,
nonchalant, nudging each other over
the sexy gravel of the spawning-beds,
the cock and the hen, in their last fettle,
ecstasy of the cloud of eggs,
ecstasy of the burst of milt,
the thrust of indomitable life.

THE GLASS

To love you in shadow as in the light
is light itself. In subterranean night
you sow the fields with fireflies of delight.

Lanarkshire holds you, under its grim grass.
But I hold what you were, like a bright glass
I carry brimming through the darkening pass.

THE DEAD

It is not true to say they are not here,
the dead. Never gone but never clear,
they punctuate the room, the street, so near

you see the eyes set deep in others' faces,
some gesture that hooks out buried embraces
of how long back: other places, other cases.

Although they are silent we know we walk with them.
There needs to be no sorry stratagem
of note or phone, wave, grin, kiss, shout, tugged hem

to feel the virtue of the undenying presence
going out and out, spreading like an essence
that fills and spills and falls and never lessens.

How can living shapes be so invaded?
The unpersuaded cannot be dissuaded –
as if the red of dead leaves never faded!

It fades, yes it goes white and skeletal
until at last there is no leaf at all,
a vein or two, a mulch, a pith, a scrawl

like this on paper which remembers it.
I ask you who are dead if it takes grit
to people shadows when the lamps are lit

in Glasgow of this old world you once knew,
or if whatever has been loved comes through
if those who want it to are still and true.

TO THE LIBRARIANS, H.W. AND H.H.

Once I began casting my life away,
books and papers waved back quick to say,
New shelves, new selves! Far from the library

I shook myself like a wet dog and barked
through water-meadows, double-rainbow-arc'd
splashes and sparkles lapped me where I larked –

A Pasternakian lightness, kicking the cumber
into others' vaults, levitating the lumber,
decimating the band but not the number –

until the hard white whistle of existence
halted me in my tracks with its insistence
on asking me if I felt no resistance

to peeling layer on layer like a flaying,
did I not hear the winds, the distant baying,
where was my life, what was Vesalius saying?

Why, there is no protection, I replied.
What you have been and done's not set aside.
Your files are you, and file through one divide.

Burn your letters, burn your boats: no tide
will ever wash away the ash you hide
of pain, or love, or pain or love denied.

ARIEL FREED

I lifted my wings at midnight.
Moonlit pines, empty paths,
broochlike lagoons dwindled below me.
Oh I was electric: my wingtips
winked like stars through the real stars.
Cold, brisk, tingling that journey,
voyage more than journey, the night
had waves, pressures I had to breast,
thrust aside, I had a figurehead or
perhaps I was a figurehead with
dolphins of the darkness as companions.
Only to have no shore, no landfall,
no runway, no eyrie, no goal and no fall!

from DEMON

A Demon

My job is to rattle the bars. It's a battle.
The gates are high, large, long, hard, black.
Whatever the metal is, it is asking to be struck.
There are guards of course, but I am very fast
And within limits I can change my shape.
The dog watches me, but I am not trying
To get out; nor am I trying to get in.
He growls if I lift my iron shaft.
I smile at that, and with a sudden whack
I drag it lingeringly and resoundingly
Along the gate; then he's berserk: fine!

The peeling miasma of the underworld
Is perfectly visible through the palings,
Grey, cold, dank, with what might be willows,
What might be villas, open caves, wildfire,
Thrones, amphitheatres, shades walking,
Shades gathering, and yes, there he is, the Orph,
The orphan, Orpheus, picking at his harp
On Pluto's glimmery piazza, the voice,
The tenderer of hope, the high-note
Shiverer of goblets, the spellbinder,
The author of what might be, surely not,
A shining wetness at the corner of Pluto's eye.
My time has come! I scramble like a monkey
From stake to stake and spar to spar and rattle
My rod, a ratchet for the rungs, a grating
Of something from gratings that has nutmegged,
Pungenced, punched, punctuated the singing

And made the singer devilish angry,
Devilish fearful, and at last devilish strong.
The vizors are after me. Too late, grey ones!
I've done my bit. Orpheus is learning along.

The Demon at the Frozen Marsh

I have been prowling round it. Nothing moves.
The winter fields are hard, half-white.
There is something fogged and hoary about
But it won't settle. I would be stiff
If I failed to circle. As it is,
My crest tingles. I am not in gloom.
The low sun paints me – I stare at it –
A sort of leaden gold along my joints.
I lift a hand spilling indescribable metal
Over the shallow crust of ice on the pond.
Is it trying to be beautiful, that sullen shine?
Nothing had better be beautiful while I am here.
If it crouches to mirror or wink at the scatter
Of washroom and watchtower and wire, it is insolent
And will not do. What are demons for?
I take my quick sharp heel and spur and smash
That shimmer to complaining splinters.
I am off to where after Oswiecim. Watch.

The Demon in Argyle Street

A ned asked me if I knew Luficer.
Never heard of him I answered, truthfully.
He scowled and kicked me, but I felt nothing.
I was hard as iron that day, on top of things.
This was in Glasgow, full of would-be demons.
It was an interesting place all the way.
The streets were thick with shadows with eyes.
I watched them trying to let nothing escape
That might be used to advantage. They watched me
Watching them watching. Well, you never know,
That was their watchword. They had never seen
A demon, a real one, but would that stop them?
Bottle from nowhere, held out, Kin ye drink it?
Ye're that thin ye kid dae wi a slurp, eh?
I drank, or at least I made them think I drank,
Wiped the bottle, handed it back with a nod.
Somehow they did not want to let me go.
The one who kicked me was still there, staring.
I waited till he blinked, then I let out
A howl that travelled from another dimension
Than any they had met with yet. It cracked
The paving-stones; echoes and shards all round.
They backed away but there was no running off.
I liked that. What could I give them?
All I could give them was a tale to tell.
I gradually vanished. They must have thought
I had jouked them, darted into the crowd.
But I was already in another place.
I left them trying out that howl of mine
To see if they could break a pavement too.

The Demon at the Brig O' Dread

I always thought the Brig o' Dread was best
For pushing people over, not for crossing.
Dread of lord or devil's not the point,
Just have it! All your smooth numpties,
Silver captains, all those suits at the bar,
There's a roaring they haven't even got cockleshells for
And it's not that far below them, not
When I'm around. They can smile like cats
But a brown spate will force their lips apart
If I can just creep, shove, tip, over they go
To flail and choke, at last understanding dread.
Oh then it's purple clamour for filing of nails!
Gulp of swaws for cars scrunching the driveway!
They were going to make a speech,
They were going to put their stamp on it,
They were going home to set their alarms
For another satisfying day of managing.
I saw we had had enough of that.
Did they think they would go on for ever?

Lean on the parapet, look for trout.
When I cowp you over, don't complain
The water is coming up to hit you
For nothing, why why why. There's no why
Except you never felt afraid till now
Or drank the dread that's worse than fear, and better.

I fish them out, just in time, lay them
Down on the verge, white, gasping, chittering
As if it would be uncontrollably
Until the life returns that they can only
Live, the second one, the little one
They'd best be cradling in their arms, and fast.

The Demon and the World

Human beings? What do you mean beings?
They have only just begun to become!
What they will be is a flicker of distant lightning.
They are my play, my joy, my matter, my mystery,
My expatriates, my exasperates, my crusty templates.
I curse them to their knees, caress them
With poppies till they dream of great others.
I carry them with me like crabbit Anchiseses – hah!
What's burning? Troy? Hell? You need asbestos?
No you don't, I am the salamander
Of the world and I snort flame like coke.
Stay with me – I said, but do they listen –
Do they hell – well, sometimes – some of them.
It is like walking on coals, that bit
Between birth and death: anyone can do it.
If they could suffer in all their lives
Even a millionth part of what I bear
Every second, they would shriek like wild things,
Break out of planes, refuse to be born.
But it is not for me to show – ever –
Even a sigh, far less a groan or a tear.
O I am the merry one, am I not?

Stations, airports: how they press in at parting,
These lovers, these partners! Is there still time?
He has taken the whistle out of his pocket,
The uniformed man. They are not quite sure
They will ever meet again, though they must say so.
Will he look back from the aircraft steps?
I don't know, I don't know. Is it far?

Anywhere is far! The poetry of departures
Jolts, grinds, judders, whines, pounds, climbs –
And then you have, alone, to get on with your life.

O they do not know what separation is!
Eternity – they think it is a fairy-tale.
I can take whatever is thrown at me
By heaven or hell; it is what is taken away
That challenges my iron and my arms.

The Demon on Algol

A common or garden angel, dead thick,
Flitting from star to star with half a robe
And a half-smile, had landed – the fool! –
On Algol, demonic caravanserai
If ever there was one, livid place, brilliant! –
It winked into space, was called the evil eye –
I liked that. I was there at my ease,
Stretched out somewhat. I had a fiery draught in me
And was high, when I saw this droopy figure
Brushing off flakes. 'All hail and all that'
I shouted, very jolly, hoisting an invisible trident.
The angel jumped so sharp it shed its rags,
Ran across the lava wailing something
In its poor piping dialect. What a coarse roar
We demons then sent after its toty buttocks
Twinkling pinkly through a rain of cinders!

A Little Catechism from the Demon

What is a demon? Study my life.
What is a mountain? Set out now.
What is fire? It is for ever.
What is my life? A fall, a call.
What is the deep? Set out now.
What is thunder? Your powder dry.
What is the film? It rolls, it tells.
What is the film? *Under the Falls.*
Where is the theatre? Under the hill.
Where is the demon? Walking the hills.
Where is the victory? On the high tops.
Where is the fire? Far in the deep.
Where is the deep? Study the demon.
Where is the mountain? Set out now.
Study my life and set out now.

The Demon Goes to Kill Death

The only way, the only way is all.
I tried the grave for size, fisted the crud,
Got handfuls of wood-pulp, gravel, grubs, teeth,
Seeds dormant and seeds dead, a trail
Of nameless black mephitic slurries.
But the one I was looking for was not there.

I tried a battlefield or two, though fields
Were few, rather the sand was fused to glass,
And oil burned screaming along the waves,
And shelled villages were smoking shells
Or hells, though the shellers crowed to heaven.
Yet the one I was looking for was not there.

I walked among the longest of the wards
Where sheets were grey and bedsores gaped and wept
And ragged families came and went, gazed
And wept, and stubbly doctors dropped asleep
By empty cupboard doors that swung and creaked.
Still the one I was looking for was not there.

She was dead white, I knew that, total white.
Her camouflage could be high mountain passes
Thick with the snow that muffled refugees
Slipping with bundles from country to no country.
Old women were silent, with bleeding feet.
But she I was looking for was not there.

I can take blizzards, I can take stench.
I will never rest till I have found her.
She is so ghastly only a demon
Would dare to grapple her and bring her down,
But bring her down I will, at the end of time
Or sooner – look – that white – O is she there?

The Demon at the Walls of Time

I ran and I ran. I was so fresh and fuelled –
The rubble of the plain hardly felt me,
Far less held me back – so filled and flash
With missionary grin and attitude
I almost laughed to find the barrier
As big in its dark burnish as they'd warned.
No top to it that I could see, no holds
Except a filigree of faint worn sculpture.
Is challenge the word or is it not?
Is it the climb of climbs, morning noon and night?

It had better be! What a wersh drag without it –
Life, I mean!
           Up it is then – careful! –
Zigzag but steady, glad to have no scree,
Not glad of useless wings, tremendous downdraught,
Nails not scrabbling – please! – but feeling and following
The life-lines of unreadable inscriptions
Cut by who by how I don't know, go
Is all I know. Beautifully far below
Now is the ground, the old brown beetly ground.
No beetles here! It's the sun and the blue
And the wall that almost everything
Seems rushing to if I dare one more look
Down, there's a sea, a clutch of cities,
Cross-hatch of rolling smoke, is it a war
Somewhere on the hot convex, I'm sure
There's war here on the wall too, written
Never to be lost, lost now, tongues, gods.
You'll not lose me so easily! I'm climbing
Into the evening until I see stars
Beyond what is only rampart rampart rampart
And if I don't I'll take the night too
And a day and a night till my crest like a shadow
(It's not a shadow though!) tops the top of the wall.

I know you can still hear me. Before I vanish:
You must not think I'll not be watching you.
I don't come unstuck. I don't give up.
I'll read the writing on the wall. You'll see.

Pelagius

I, Morgan, whom the Romans call Pelagius,
Am back in my own place, my green Cathures
By the frisky firth of salmon, by the open sea
Not far, place of my name, at the end of things
As it must seem. But it is not a dream
Those voyages, my hair grew white at the tiller,
I have been where I say I have been,
And my cheek still burns for the world.
That sarcophagus by the Molendinar –
Keep the lid on, I am not stepping into it yet!
I used to think of the grey rain and the clouds
From my hot cave in the Negev, I shooed
The scuttle of scorpions. I had a hat –
You should have seen me – against the sun
At its zenith in that angry Palestine.
I spoke; I had crowds; there was a demon in me.
There had been crowds four centuries before,
And what had come of that? That was the question.
I did not keep back what I had to say.
Some were alarmed. They did not like my red hair.
But I had a corps of friends who shouldered
Every disfavour aside, took ship with me
Westward over the heaving central sea.
We came to Carthage then, and not alone.
The city was seething livid with refugees.
Such scenes, such languages! Such language!
The Goths were in Rome. I saw a master
I had studied under, wild-eyed,
Clutching tattered scrolls, running.
I saw a drift of actors with baskets
Brimming broken masks, they gestured

Bewildered beyond any mime.
I saw a gladiator with half a sword.
I heard a Berber's fiddle twang like the end of a world.
Morgan, I said to myself, take note,
Take heart. In a time of confusion
You must make a stand. There is a chrysalis
Throbbing to disgorge oppression and pessimism,
Proscription, prescription, conscription,
Praying mantises. Cut them down!

One stood against me:
Distinguished turncoat, ex-Manichee, ex this and that,
Preacher of chastity with a son in tow,
A Christian pistoned by new-found fervour,
Born of the desert sand in occupied land,
Born my exact coeval but not my coadjutor,
Bishop in Hippo brandishing anathemas,
Bristling with intelligence not my intelligence,
Black-hearted but indefatigable –
Augustine! You know who you are
And I know who you are and we shall die
Coeval as we came to life coeval.
We are old. The dark is not far off.
It is four hundred years now since those nails
Were hammered in that split the world
And not just flesh. Text and anti-text
Crush the light. You can win,
Will win, I can see that, crowd me out
With power of councils, but me –
Do you know me, can you believe
I have something you cannot have –
My city, not the city of God –
It is to come, and why, do you know why?

Because no one will believe without a splash from a font
Their baby will howl in eternal cold, or fire,
And no one will suffer the elect without merit
To lord it over a cringing flock, and no one
Is doomed by Adam's sin to sin for ever,
And who says Adam's action was a sin,
Or Eve's, when they let history in.

Sometimes when I stand on Blythswood Hill
And strain my eyes (they are old now) to catch
Those changing lights of evening, and the clouds
Going their fiery way towards the firth,
I think we must just be ourselves at last
And wait like prophets – no, not wait, work! –
As prophets do, to see the props dissolve,
The crutches, threats, vain promises,
Altars, ordinances, comminations
Melt off into forgetfulness.
My robe flaps; a gull swoops; man is all.
Cathurian towers will ring this hill.
Engines unheard of yet will walk the Clyde.
I do not even need to raise my arms,
My blessing breathes with the earth.
It is for the unborn, to accomplish their will
With amazing, but only human, grace.

Merlin

What time, what year, what universe, all's one.
I have been seen in crowded courts and in fields
And by long roads and on great waters.
No one knows where to have me, but
Who is there who does not know of me?
I made some rough magic for King Roderick.
He fed me in his court on Dumbarton Rock.
He pleased me in his palace at Partick.
He took me to talk to his countryman
Kentigern whom I took to as well as talked to
As we bantered over a beaker the difference
Between the miraculous and the maroculous.
Good days those, out of many not good!
Men went to war; Roderick went; I went.
I am no fighter, why should I go?
'Record my victory,' said Roderick.
'You are a bard. Sing me.' Sing what?

The victory of death, the cries, the rolling limbs,
Clang of swords and reddening of grass,
The pain that rises to the grand indifference
Of clouds as they muffle past, the fury
That hunts the pain that hunts the clouds –
All that, but then I watched the head of a friend
Bounce down the hill, blood path, not bearable.

Battles end, and surgeons come, and ravens.
A horn blew truce, but nothing could console me.
Was I to sing that a king had won?
War wins wounds, widows, it eclipses the sun
For many. I could only run,
I wailed, roared, tore my tunic, tore myself

From every restraining hand, took to the wilds,
Half mad, or mad indeed as some men said,
Tunnelling into the Caledonian forest.

How long did I live there? What is time?
I became a green man, a man of the woods,
My beard grew, I ate roots and nuts,
I had mulberries and rain for my dinner.
Only the wolf, grey wolf, dear wolf
Was mine to roam the thickets with.
Best of companions, better than man,
You followed me who had nothing to give,
Your hair was white with age, you limped,
You stretched beside me, howling faintly
Under the cold leaves and the constellations.

Those who found me came softly, playing lutes.
They put my wasted body on a litter,
Carried me back into humanity.
I held the burning eyes of the wolf
Till the very last moment. The madness was gone,
And now I must make the most of men.

I am living here in my house of glass
On Cathkin Hill, above the twinkling lights
Of Cathures with its sweet green hollows.
It is not glass, not smoke, not even air
But has its own dimension. My sister Gwen
Helps me in my observatory.
I am told she is like Ada, Byron's daughter,
Mathematician before her time.
With our double vision we untwist binary stars.
A light kiss then, and do we have phantom supper?
Do you think we would tell you! Naw naw,

As they say in Cathures. We donate our spirit
To that gallus city. We are quicksilver
With no mould to run into. Watch us change.
This glass house which is not made of glass
Is Merlin's esplumoir, his moulting-cage
Where high above the rambling Molendinar
He waits until the new enchanter
Flashes a more formidable feather
And that, too, not for ever.

George Fox

All right, it was time to be a pilgrim.
Dreary Middle England I got through,
Rode a poor horse and sold it, bought a better,
Steaming and shivering under the wild trees
In drasty weather, devilish wet,
Handful of oats, knuckle of cheese,
Waiting for gale to dwindle to breeze,
Praying a bit but only a bit,
Gerrup, Silver! and George get off your knees!
It's no more than another moor or two,
How many lines of thorny wind-bent hedge –
And please, no foxy metaphors about thorns,
We're pilgrims all, sure, no sweat, no crowns,
It presses on my temples without blood,
The earth, the folk who cry or do not cry –
Where was I? oh yes, going north,
It's only miles, curlews, lead-mines, ruins,
Sheep in the crumbling keep, rabbits asleep –
Until I followed the dull shine
Of the Clyde rolling fish-full and dark
Towards the towers of that dark

Place, that Glasgow, where I must fish
For souls, oh, splash them into light.

I have preached the word, and a good word it is,
In fields and market-squares and meeting-houses.
Sometimes sullen faces glum up at me,
Or sceptic sneers lurking on the sidelines.
What in God's name (God forgive me!) is wrong
With the people of Glasgow who have not even the wit
To be sullen, far less the chutzpah to sneer?
Admittedly I arrived somewhat dusty
At one of the city gates, I was not dapper,
Uncouth was the word no doubt,
Suspicious the alien vocables of Leicestershire!
The grim guard took me to the magistrate.
I kept my hat on as I always do.
Men of authority are men of straw.
I was polite and he was polite.
Perhaps he thought me mad, but harmless.
I was at liberty, he said, to hold a meeting
In the town centre, open to all.
Well, I have had meetings and meetings,
A hundred folk, a dozen, even five,
But never till now have I had none.
Not one, no, not a single soul,
Not a child, not even a dog
Came to listen to the best of news
They would ever hear in this life,
In this city, in this vale of darkness.

Were they all too busy making money?
Were they stuffing their stores with calico and claret?
Were they bent over balances, or boosting their buildings?
Were they bolting salmon and slapping their bellies?

Were they raging and searching for runaway slaves?
Their trades and their trons and their trappings are trash.
Is it gold you want to stash?
All that brilliant bullion?
Bullion is ash!

I could deliver nothing in that place.
I was shot of Glasgow, I came away.
I say I was shot of that Glasgow!
Pedlar Satan can pad up and open his case.

Vincent Lunardi

I do not know what is wrong with me.
I am sick, I lie like lead on this bed.
The sisters took me in. I hear their bells
And the dull rumour of Lisbon beyond these walls.
I am so poor I have nothing.
I have nothing and I am nothing.
The world has shrunk to a bowl of gruel
When the sun goes down. Another world
Is not yet closed, my memories.
I summon them and they come running.
Why can I not rise to greet them?
To rise was my life, I was born for it!

I still remember that early dream of flight.
Playing in the olive groves of Lucca
I stretched my arms to match the dragonflies,
Buzzed and zigzagged like a bee, but most,
Oh most and best, I watched the summer swallow
Slicing the air with a rapture I gave to it

From my own longing. I would have the air,
I would have it someday!
                          Twenty years ago
The air was indeed mine, I was an aeronaut –
I was not the first, I don't claim that, but
I was noted, I was marked, I was famous,
I was loved, I was honoured, I was fêted
In England and Scotland, Italy and Spain,
Even in dusty Portugal where I am dying.
But I am not talking about death!
I am talking about life and life abundant!
I have enough breath to spell it.
Memory breaks the sound barrier.
We are off and away, back to happy Glasgow
Where I rose twice from the dead
Tussocks of Glasgow Green and made a wonder.
The hydrogen roared, the flaccid silk blossomed
To a great pod of pink and yellow and green
Stretched taut and shimmering into the blue.
I leapt into the decorated basket,
Decorative myself if I may say so,
Dressed in my regimental colours –
Neapolitan if you want to know –
With a good leg, many ladies commend it,
Waving my flag and blowing my speaking-trumpet
While a band blared the most rousing of marches,
Bells were pealed, and the people waved
To my waving, and exclaimed and shouted and whistled
From tens of thousands of upturned faces
As my six-men-high balloon majestically
Lifted above that ever-living city.
Do you think I cut a figure, cut a dash
In that airy cabin, in my stockings of silk,
My lacy cuffs, my goffered cravat, my – ah,

That hat! – was I not gay that day
And was it not the gayest of days?
The ladies thought so: some clapped, some fainted,
All had eyes for the aeronaut. Do you know
Some of them later helped me to patch
A rent in the balloon, and I gave them
A thread or two of silk: some said
It would become a locket in their bosoms.
Why do I say these things? I had no lady.
I danced a minuet, kissed here and there.
But my only bride was the high air.

I wonder who will remember Lunardi
That soared among the clouds and saw below him
Trongate and Tontine, and the Saracen's Head
Where he lodged and talked the night into pleasure?
It is like a dream of the gay times
That are possible and to be so cherished
We have a little comfort to be taken
As the shadows close in. They do, they do.
It is cold too. Who is that standing in the door?

A GULL

A seagull stood on my window-ledge today,
said nothing, but had a good look inside.
That was a cold inspection I can tell you!
North winds, icebergs, flash of salt
crashed through the glass without a sound.
He shifted from leg to leg, swivelled his head.
There was not a fish in the house – only me.
Did he smell my flesh, that white one? Did he think
I would soon open the window and scatter bread?
Calculation in those eyes is quick.
'I tell you, my chick, there is food *everywhere*.'
He eyed my furniture, my plants, an apple.
Perhaps he was a mutation, a supergull.
Perhaps he was, instead, a visitation
which only used that tight firm forward body
to bring the waste and dread of open waters,
foundered voyages, matchless predators,
into a dry room. I knew nothing.
I moved; I moved an arm. When the thing saw
the shadow of that, it suddenly flapped,
scuttered claws along the sill, and was off,
silent still. Who would be next for those eyes,
I wondered, and were they ready, and in order?

GASOMETER

You don't care about the wildness of the sky,
my old gasometer! The kitchen window
frames your gaunt frame, the black cross-struts
stand firm, stand out, unyielding to the passion
of reds and purples in the dying day.
I have seen your stark ring taking sunlight
till you were something molten, vanishing,
magical – and when the moment passed
you were strong and dark as your dead hammermen.
(They whistle in the long-gone sheds. Listen!)
You cannot hide where your strength comes from.
You are constructivist to the core.
Did you want gargoyles to crouch in your angles?
I don't think so. Yours is the art of use.
You could be painted, floodlit, archeologized,
but I prefer the unremitting stance
of what you were in what you are, no more.
You are an iron guard or talisman,
and I hear that those who talk of eyesores
you have consigned, bless you, to the bad place.

Day of tearing down, day of recycling,
wait a while! Let the wind whistle
through those defenceless arms and the moon bend
a modicum of its glamorous light upon
you, my familiar, my stranded hulk – a while!

THE FRESHET

Will you not brush me again, rhododendron?
You were blowsy with rainwater when you drenched my cheek,
I might have been weeping, but was only passing, too
quickly! You were so heavy and wet and fresh
I thought your purple must run, make me a Pict.
You made yourself a sponge for me, I got
a shower, a shot, a spray, a freshet, a headstart
and then I was away from you. I can't go back.
I can't go back, you know, retrace my steps,
tilt my other cheek out like an idiot,
stumble purposefully against the blooms
for another heady shiver. I want it though!

One day when I am not thinking, walking
steadily past house and garden, measuring
the traffic lights, you will reach out, won't you,
at a corner, toppling over railings
just to see me, crowd of mauve raindrops
shaking and bursting, mauling me gently
with your petal paws, shock of the petal,
shock of the water, I am waiting for that,
out of I don't care how many pavements,
black railings, and the darkly breathing green.

BLIND

Almost unconscionably sweet
Is that voice in the city street.
Her fingers skim the leaves of braille.
She sings as if she could not fail
To activate each sullen mind
And make the country of the blind
Unroll among the traffic fumes
With its white stick and lonely rooms.
Even if she had had no words,
Unsentimental as a bird's
Her song would rise in spirals through
The dust and gloom to make it true
That when we see such fortitude,
Though she cannot, the day is good.

AT EIGHTY

Push the boat out, compañeros,
Push the boat out, whatever the sea.
Who says we cannot guide ourselves
through the boiling reefs, black as they are,
the enemy of us all makes sure of it!
Mariners, keep good watch always
for that last passage of blue water
we have heard of and long to reach
(no matter if we cannot, no matter!)
in our eighty-year-old timbers
leaky and patched as they are but sweet,
well seasoned with the scent of woods
long perished, serviceable still

in unarrested pungency
of salt and blistering sunlight. Out,
push it all out into the unknown!
Unknown is best, it beckons best,
like distant ships in mist, or bells
clanging ruthless from stormy buoys.

THE FERRY

Now here is a pleasantly crowded picture:
breezy summer, sun on hulls, harbour gulls,
you can almost hear the engines chugging –
but don't be distracted from the central figure.
He looks like one of the roughs, but is he?
His light blue shirt is open to the waist.
Casual, that's it. His heavy-lidded eyes
are brooding on the beautiful bahookie
of a lounger on the rail of the Brooklyn ferry.
It is Walt, of course it is, who else,
of Manhattan the son, loafing as usual,
old camerado, trolling for images
to put in his book, and *who touches this book*
touches a man, so as the picture shows
he is carrying his *Leaves of Grass* in his pocket
and hoping that somebody will touch him.

LOVE AND A LIFE

Those and These

Frank, Jean, Cosgrove, John, Malcolm, Mark – loves of sixty years
Were a life that disported itself in many wonders not dispirited, though fears
Visited often, and were there not (said Mark) other dears
Like Leila who clutched your crotch in Cairo in '41, she just disappears
Is that it? And the night you broke the bed out there (said Malcolm), too many
    beers –
      Are you airbrushing a face,
      A grace, a disgrace –
No no I'm not, they are all there, crowding round me, others, milling, mingling,
    tingling, tangling, pinning me, pulling my ears.

Freeze-Frame

None of those once known is disknown, hidden, lost, I see them in clouds in
    streets in trees
Often and often, or in dreams, or if I feel I ought to be at my ease
They prod and probe: 'When my head was on your knees
And your hand was on my head, did you think time would seize
Head, hand, all, lock all away where there is no ring of keys –?'
      I did not, oh I did not,
      But look what I have got,
Frame of a moment made for friendless friendly time to freeze.

222

The Top

What use is a picture when the universe is up and drumming
With its passions motions missions misprisions relentlessly going and coming
Ghostly file of memories mopping and mowing and mumming –
In their hands a brilliant top that they lash and lash to release its humming –
It spins whistling softly until it wobbles, and you speed it with one last angry
       thumbing
       But soon it must fall back
       Into silence, attack
As you will, take the lash as you will, to stave off the mundane numbing and
       dumbing.

Tracks and Crops

Memory is not a top that never stops, but there is such a top, top of the tops,
Call it a world, it's drenched with what you did, it grins and groans with the
       drips and drops
Of your life, the sweat the blood the wine the weeping the honey and the hops,
Whatever you squeezed or poured or distilled or scrambled from pores or
       veins, elixirs, poisons, potions not filched from shops –
A bloom or glow like the first faint stirring of earthly unearthly crops –
       The cosmic harvesters
       Are scouring the universe
For sheafs and tracks of love left well by all from lucky you to luckless but
       once-loved horny veggie triceratops.

Jurassic

I have a dinosaur egg in my cupboard, hard, heavy, fused to the rock it haunts.
Someday Mark will have it and tempt its Jurassic chirp with his shazams and
    taunts.
Love laid the egg even in those armoured times when the bellows and vaunts
Of the laithly saurians belted out their ancient unlaithly wants –
(And tenderly our own dear crocodile conveys her squeaking brood in jaws no
    buffalo daunts) –
      Some malice surely must
      Have sent the deadly dust
That smothers what the pregnant earth gigantically flags up and flaunts.

Crocodiles

Patient patient men who can make pets of crocodiles
Disclaim they have degrees in sedation or access to preternatural wiles.
'It's touch,' they say. 'If you know where to press, that's good; if not, not! There
    are no smiles
(Don't be misled!), no purrs, no contented sighs to help you. Forget the styles
Of furry bundles. Communicate far back and down, then further back and
    further down, eras, miles.
      Expressionlessness
      Has ports of ingress –
Enter, clasp, hug, and then how quickly the esteemed veneer resiles!'

Touch

Touch is everything or nearly everything or it is nothing. Crocodiles mate, after
    all.
The Devil's swedger at minus a hundred is as cold and as ruthless as the Pole
And only the most despairing and abandoned, female or male, could take it in
    their hole
Or so we were told, or so they were told, when wretched creatures were taught of
    the Fall
Of Man instead of the Rise of Man and hair-shirts and chastity-belts were
    thought to assist our feeble but our dearest soul
        Which struggled, crying, to be free
        And use its body to be
The means of greatest grace, frolicking and fucking in the tropical throbbing
    unstoppable waterfall.

Night Hunt

The waters fall, and under the steelbright moon the hunters and the hunted
    shake the shadows in their trackless well-tracked wood.
The barred and silvered dark is like a gateless cage crammed full of living food.
Food for living! It cowers but you have to snatch it, crunch it, get it down your
    throat for good.
Who can say blameworthy bloodweltering nature is anxious to be understood?
Well, nothing is worthy of blame that feeds the root of bud baby and brood.
        It's a darkness all the same,
        Coming to light in the shame
Of knowing we would probably not banish our misgivings, even if we could.

Under the Falls

Break through and down with you, lovers all, down but not dry behind the falls.
You're staring into a rainbow spray, an unstrung bead-curtain as ready to brush
     breasts as any in cool levantine halls.
The loud fresh swish and rush, the flash, the drizzle disorientates as well as
     enthrals.
You sit back in a limbo cave of wonder, imagining the bird-calls
Whistling through a paradise garden where all that falls
     Is a loved footfall
     Hardly disturbing at all
The green and drowsy floor, and a world stretches somewhere, unseen, without
     woes or walls.

An Early Garden

My grandmother had a garden where I played as if arrayed in the heady scents
     of other days –
Sweet pea mignonette wallflower phlox – recollection sees them shining in
     rainless summer rays
Blooming and wafting for ever, and in the absence of roses demanding special
     praise.
I remember roses much later, but in that early garden their erotic blaze
Would have broken the innocence of such a mixed sweet haze
     When I dreamed of lands
     Untouched by hands
And drifted along even greater multi-scented ways where nothing, except a
     lucky memory, stays.

A Garden Lost

Maud never came into the garden: the fool was ower blate!
She thought the poet's deep voice and floppy hat were great
But oh, the garden was squishy with worms and slugs and pigeons would mate
Before her eyes and a cobwebby shed would relate
Either silence or old horrors. Well, one day they padlocked the gate
    And she looked in and cried
    'Oh I could have tried!'
But love is not invited twice and longing comes too late.

Beyond the Garden

When they lock the garden you go out into tumbleweed and sidewinder land.
You stumble a bit, curse a bit, thirst a bit until you see you have to settle into the
    ways of sand.
Date palms and desert springs, find them; eat lizards; understand
Every dust-devil may disgorge an afreet, no demon is banned
In the wilderness; keep watch; keep sane. Dunes, yes, on this strand
    But they don't show you a sea
    And you must learn to be
As dry as a scorpion, or a burr in the sand-golden tresses of Fand.

Cape Found

After how many days, how many months, we heard the waves, and sand became
     rock, and rock fell into the sound
So far below we hesitated but did call it Cape Found.
It was a great bay full of whales blowing. From our cliff the whole earth seemed
     round.
We clambered down to the machair and jumped on the springy half-soaked
     blessed ground.
'Do you remember the *Heiliger Dankgesang*?' 'Bits.' 'Sing some.' The frail notes
     rose and crowned
    Our passage back to men,
    To women, to children,
To ships and sails of health, to the whale's road, the gull's acres, brilliant, bonded
     and sound.

Jean

If you think it is easy to be in love, you have misheard.
Jean said yes to the war; she had a very Latin word
About coming back with your shield or on it, assumed with justice that I would
     be undeterred.
Left me with an old red ring, a last kiss, and many letters I could reread even
     when ever so slightly beer-slurred
In my sweltering troopship bound for shores where other loves were not to be
     ignored.
    I hear her ringing laugh
    Cut through the draff and chaff
Like a knife-edge and after six decades I smile as I bend to burnish my word-
     hoard.

War Voyage

A poet in a troopship – is it to the ends of the earth? – wake the anchor –
Hundreds of hammocks swaying and snoring – time for ribaldries, no space for
      rancour –
Lashings of rain at first as we passed a ghostly rain-shrouded tanker –
South then, south round Africa, months of sweat, daily deck drills to make us
      leaner and lanker –
Near Suez, admonitory slides in close-up of ever kind and colour of chancre –
      Water-watchers all
      Through sun and through squall
In case some sleekit dark sub from Kiel should pull an eerie flanker.

In Sidon

Cosgrove my closest companion that burning year on the Lebanese coast,
I have written about you already but raise you this last toast.
Nothing happened between us and that might seem a boast
Since there is pain in silence, but I never deserted the post
Of our vibrant daily intimacies even if the best and the worst
      Tore me for all to see
      Eyes down in decency.
So it was good, and I tell you this, I see you, your image is clear, you are in my
      mind, you have not grown old, my Cosgrove, you are no ghost!

An Encounter 1

Those possible worlds that we see and cannot alter – oh they are a devastation!
The man beside me on the plane with his short-sleeved safari jacket needed no
      persuasion
To talk: we were friends, brothers, long before we reached the destination.
His wife on his other side was a mouse, never spoke: she was not part of an
      equation
That in word and look, hand on sleeve, pressed knee proved an instant mutual
      one-hour-long revelation
      Of impossible desire
      Which could only expire
As we took our separate ways on the tarmac, nursing elation, fighting desolation.

An Encounter 2

(In another universe, I poisoned her coffee and fled with Chuck to Amsterdam
Where we made some disguise and jumped onto a jangling tram
And snuggled into a brown café to smoke a little something and down the odd
      dram
And climbed to a steep high narrow room and lay there trying to cram
A lifetime into a night, pausing only to look down across the Dam
      And the dark canal
      Where even the banal
Quiver of a floating moon we took as a glory and in that universe, briefly, we
      were happy, without a qualm.)

Desire

It is a power, it is a mystery, it is a fate, but above all it is a power.
The jaws of Venus will not let go their pray. Hour after hour
They sink deeper, and the victim even smiles to see the spreading flower
Of blood, as it springs from those scary threshings of life. Don't cower,
Don't wince! It's only a nightmare, it's only a movie, it's only imaginary Phaedra
    shrieking from her tower.
    'Only, only' you cry?
    What do you want to deny?
Are you trying to tell us all these flecks of blood are not from something
    struggling to be born? You think it's like the passing sting of some damned
    April shower?

Love

Love rules. Love laughs. Love marches. Love is the wolf that guards the gate.
Love is the food of music, art, poetry. It fills us and fuels us and fires us to create.
Love is terror. Love is sweat. Love is bashed pillow, crumpled sheet, unenviable
    fate.
Love is the honour that kills and saves and nothing will ever let that high
    ambiguity abate.
Love is the crushed ice that tingles and shivers and clinks fidgin-fain for the
    sugar-drenched absinth to fall on it and alter its state.
    With love you send a probe
    So far from the globe
No one can name the shoals the voids the belts the zones the drags the flares it
    signals all to leave all and to navigate.

After a Lecture

Last and most unexpected friend, do you know you overthrew me
In those first moments when you walked towards me in that lecture-room, not
    to undo me
But you did undo me, I was shaking, I felt that well-known spear go through me,
And when we talked my mind was racing like a computer to keep that contact
    sparking. What drew me
Was irreducible but recognisable – drythroat fragments, physical certainties,
    emanations and invasions so quick to imbue me
        And wound me with hope
        I swore I would cope
With whatever late late lifeline this man, whom I knew I loved, picked up and
    threw me.

Plans

Mark, here we are, here we go, let us celebrate four years of letters and talk,
Purdey and Dostoevsky and Glenmorangie and a splash of Pasolini will never be
    out of stock
I assure you, and although when you are in Italy it is true I may watch the clock
For your safe return, there is nothing north or south that is able to block
Our invisible communication. With it we shall live to unlock
    Something quite sizable
    Perhaps inadvisable! –
Oh I don't know what, leave it for the shock, we don't want anything to scatter
    off at half-cock.

Brickies

Scaffolding rises like a forest round the six storeys of Whittingehame Court.
The metal poles are hammered into place, the planks are laid, the brickies are at
their sport
Of scampering up the near-vertical ladders, our fort
Bristles with a bantering excrescence of life which is, well, art of a sort.
'For a full picture,' you said, 'for the full Brueghel we need female brickies in
skirts – short!'
'They'd have jeans,' I said,
'So keep a cool head.'
'Use your imagination, man. That hoot from the Clyde! It's a boatload of feisty
busty brickies getting their black-leather-skirted arse into port!'

Italy

You'll be in Florence now, my man, and is there scaffolding on the *duomo*, or
only history and the sun?
Ghostly Etruscan backchat even before the city was begun?
A whiff of Savonarola? Or are pigeons with cameras the new smoking gun
To show that tourism rules, obliterates, takes a story that will run and run
And runs with it, high art, dropping a dim litter of Goth and Hun?
Tell me when you come back.
I'm peering through a crack
In the dusty polythene at distant Italy, and you, where you may be, what you will
do, what you have done.

Whistling

What a blessing it is when you have memories that sustain you
Through absence and distance that otherwise would drain you
Of hope and therefore of will! Love will never not pain you
But at the end of pain there is someone who will not disdain you
And a slipstream of joy from Glasgow to Firenze can hardly contain you
       As you break the clouds
       To jostle the crowds
Where Mark might be whistling a snatch or a catch that would carelessly care
       for you and sain you.

Harry

– Tell us about Harry. – Harry the vanman? – The very man. Go ahead.
– Where shall I begin? He delivered newspapers and the van was red.
– That's not too interesting. – We used to play strip draughts before we went to
       bed.
We lit out for the Blackpool Illuminations instead of trolling the Med.
I am sure there are many other things that might be said.
       – So he's not a fixture?
       I get the picture.
– Do you? I don't think so. Wayward paths can be affectionately led.

The Last Dragon

Is it the mists of autumn? My mind's dislodged, far back, far off, in turmoil, a
    memory trail
To the grizzled warrior in Heorot hall whose heart *inne weoll*
Thonne he wintrum frod worn gemunde and told his ancient tale.
I too am old in winters and stories and may I never fail
To guard my word-hoard before the dragon with his flailing tail
    Sweeps everything away
    Leaves nothing to say
Either in turmoil or in peace, and neither poetry nor song nor all their longing
    can avail.

Dragon on Watch

My grandmother's bronze dragon straddles my mantelpiece like a guard,
Heavy, fierce, Chinese, and now quite old, he shows no sign of not being hard
If activated. I have just been dusting his tongue which licks out like a flame.
    Fine, unmarred,
His ears and horns are flames, his tail is flames, his arched reptilian back is
    unscarred.
He will certainly outlive me, but to eat me – that's barred!
    He can watch over Mark
    When I am in the dark.
Polish him with respect, with a dry cloth, and the house will never be ill-starred.

Scan Day

Two scans in one day, CT and bone – they are certainly looking after me.
Computerised tomography like a non-invasive Vesalius will slice me apart to see
If I am really what I ought to be and not what I don't want to be.
In the giant redwood forest you are shown the rings of a fallen tree
With the few blips and wavy bits that tell you it's been a good fight, even with
     destiny.
          There are no chimeras
          Under the cameras.
You are laid out as you are, imperfect, waiting, wondering, approximately free.

Skeleton Day

Bizarrely brought, demanding thought, the benedictions of the bone scan!
There you lie, well-injected, clothed but motionless man
As the machine lowers its load close over you and begins its creeping pan
Downwards, while the screen unrolls a little skeleton, a blueprint, a plan –
That plan is you! Skull, ribs, hips emerge from the dark like a caravan
          Bound for who knows where
          Stepping through earth or air
Still of a piece and still en route, beating out the music of tongs and bones while
     it can.

236

October Day

Get the sun out, get it shining! It's only October, and only a tenth of the leaves
      are yellowing.
Prod a few white clouds out of their beds and get them billowing!
We can sit a while and not batten down the hatches for a gale following.
We can clink a glass and swirl the wine and still not rush the swallowing.
We can smoke in a moveless dear afternoon till the late light spreads its
      hallowing
        Over everything
        And then we must bring
The day to rest with good ease, recollections, far thoughts, love and dallying.

Titania

Scratch him between the ears, he is in excellent fettle, and when he listens to the
      tongs and bones
He nods his head, brays gently in time, and his hurdy-gurdy drones
Ravish Titania who has fled from pavanes and protocols trumpets and thrones
To be with her beast, to cuddle her cuddy, to dawdle with her donkey, to
      translate his tones
Into transports of love. So why is it touching? You don't need erogenous zones
        For a parable of affection
        Doomed in direction
But groping for the gold that's panned from gainless pains and groans.

Tatyana

Tatyana sat at her little window table in the moonlight.
First love forbade her even to ask whether it was wise to write.
Her nightgown slipped from her shoulder as she made her heart naked all that
   long night.
Her letter fell dead. Onegin thought her naïve, provincial, and not very bright.
Bright enough to marry money, but glittering at a ball, poised and mature in the
   candlelight,
   She knew that happiness
   Was really something else,
Was once *tak vozmozhno, tak blizko*, so possible, so near, and now only
   remembered, receded, almost out of sight.

Teresa

Up here in Ávila, and grand the sierra, there's so much air and space for vision.
God must be nearer by a sky or two. It burns. He burns. And there is no
   remission.
There's love, and love, and then there's love – and love – and if you are really
   aflame, who makes the decision?
I'm a bustler, I'm a hustler, I'm a hussy, I have a mission, I make an incision, I
   court collision.
Who do I love? My barefoot sisters, Juan de la Cruz who might be my son, the
   intuition
   I have of one divine
   Lover who will be mine
But not till I die. Ah, *muero porque no muero!* God forgive my ardent impatient
   admission!

John 1

Nothing will bring him back. I know that, of course I know that. The days
When I do not think of him are few, but if I turn my gaze
On a phantom, on a plot of earth, on a faded photograph of great times, I raise
Nothing, nearly nothing, no, not nothing, it is the something of a pain that stays
Ineradicable and only to be mitigated when I breathe the phrase
     I loved you. You must know
     It was truly so, although
As clay in clay you cannot catch my thanks, my steadiness, my lateness, my
     praise.

John 2

Once you dyed your greying hair with a black marker and the pillow was a mess.
What did I care? What did you care? We were in such happiness
It might have been peach pink or saltire blue. And as for dress
My flares were wider than yours – oh no they weren't – oh yes they were –
     confess!
Faffing along the scorching Black Sea coast we were burnt too raw to caress.
     At Constantsa we were blest
     By a breeze from the west
Unforgiving Ovid stared down at us, but even in that half-decayed port we could
     not share a smidgen of his distress.

When in Thrace

Ovid had to start wearing furs – layers of them sometimes – in Thrace.
He said the winter winds and the salt sleet would cut off your face.
He threeped and threeped that his exile was a conspiracy and a disgrace.
Surrealistic metamorphoses of love and lust were hardly to be written about in
     that place.
But once he learned to stop girning and moaning he uncovered a trace
     Of common humanity
     Cast off urbanity
Wrote poems in the barbarian tongue which he hated but which was now, as a
     philosopher would one day say, the case.

Lust

Lust is a languorous pot of fumes in the hallway. Lust is steam-pistons. Lust is
     promises promises.
Lust is a bead-curtain chinkled by a dancer's nipples as she shakes and shines
     through the teasing interstices.
Lust rides the wildebeest into oblivion. On its back are princes, blisters,
     mistresses.
Lust is the corer screwing and sloshing its juicy cock-shaped tunnel into the
     melon of your wishes.
Lust is the holding of a sweaty glance across the gay disco's heaving dance-floor
     and its bareback vistas.
     It is really not very good
     And we don't think you should
But we know you will. Dinners come brimming from the kitchen and you grin
     as you crunch the ashes from those hot hot dishes.

Late Day

There are days when, and there are days if, and then again there are simply days.
After a long night, after a bad night, the sun did let out a few rays
That filtered gamely through the grimy scaffolding. The poor wintry stuff gets
    my praise.
If darkness kept the world like a closed eye, we could only get our nightmare to
    search and gaze
From its rolling red and bridled eyeball as we ride it down and down where
    muzzles never graze.
      How great the winter sun
      When horrors are undone
By gentlest flimsiest fingers lighting our fingers as we open the curtains on a day
    content to glimmer and not to blaze.

Bobby

Bobby on one elbow, stretched out in his red jeans on my carpet, thirty years ago
Bobby at the Grand Canyon, squinting up, on the verge, fathomless purple
    below
Bobby a bundle of nerves as the transatlantic plane comes down to land, heavy
    and slow
Bobby mugged, compensated, an unexpected few thousands to blow
Bobby with a stick and a cap and a fluttery heart in a basement café in our
    Glasgow
      Where we faithfully meet
      Take the lift to the street
Having swirled out our foamy chocolate-sprinkled late but oh not last
    cappuccino!

G.

'Ah canny say Ah love ye but.' 'I know, that's all right, it's all right.'
'Ah love ma wife an ma weans. Ah don't go aroon thinkin aboot you day an
    night.
Ah wahnt tae come in yir mooth, an see thae teeth a yours – see they don't bite!
Ah like ye right enough, but aw that lovey-dovey stuff is pure shite.
Ah widny kiss ye, God no.' But kiss me he did one afternoon, with a drink in
    him, at Central Station, on the lips, in broad daylight.
      It will not be denied
      In this life. It is a flood-tide
You may dam with all your language but it breaks and bullers through and
    blatters all platitudes and protestations before it, clean out of sight.

Tomtits

Two twinkling tomtits were enjoying the scaffolding outside my window. Did
    they think it was a tree?
Surely they are not going to nest in those hard angles for all the world to see?
Against the filthy struts the sodden planks the louring sky they are new-minted
    fresh and free,
Flashing flirting blue and yellow, dark eyes darting missing nothing, not even
    me! –
A pair, an item, a unit, so magnetic to each other and so beautiful to us that we
    say they must be
      In love, what else could wind
      The springs of heart and mind
To frisk through all that muck and murk in such precarious liberty?

Arabian Night

The runners through the darkness hear the hooves, is it behind them or all
    round?
They are inured to the unknown and only wonder idly at the sound.
They track the stony desert to bring back the bride, all braided and bound
With silver and leather, silent, white-veiled and white-gowned.
Why did one of them not hunker down and set his ear to the ground?
        Jealous riders jumped them
        Sabred them and dumped them
But the bright bride had learned to hide, stripped off her braws, put on her
    shades, called her maids, packed a van and roared off, never to be found.

November Night

Dark and darker the year, late leaves flying, my thoughts turning
Back to '38, war looming, lectures distracting, feelings racing, engrossing,
    burning,
Jean and Frank together within me smouldering shouldering laughing tugging
    churning,
Frank the first, king of something, emerging, emulating, energising, a whole
    province of yearning,
Gallus Russianist, stocky communist, quick-talking anti-somnambulist, your
    learning
        Was my learning, but then
        You were the first of men
In that impossible dimension of love which now with unspoken groans and even
    secret tears I was approaching and discerning.

Spanish Night

And yet, *en una noche oscura*, as we know from the words of swarthy much-
    buffeted John of the Cross,
In the darkest night, from a dungeon, a real one, rich in hideous shit and chains
    and slime and moss,
It is not impossible to bribe a jailer and bamboozle his guttering god like a joss,
Escaping from dark into dark but leaving great doctors to gloss
What light he saw then in the stars he sent his thankful, his hot, his loving
    thoughts across.
    He sank onto the breast
    Of one whom he loved best
Delirious among the dim night lilies where at last there was neither loved nor
    lover, but there was love and everything that was not love was dross.

Whatever Happened To

the young man sitting next to me in the Biograph (peace to its long-lost
    rubble!), in that smoky place
Where it was too dark to take stock of anybody's face,
Who seized my wandering hand, laid it flat palm upwards, and with his index
    finger started to trace
I.L.O.V.E.Y.O.U., clear as if he had spoken, letter by steady letter, crossing with
    quick grace
My life-line and my heart-line and moving into a space
    He was not blate to invade
    But was he then afraid
Scurrying off as if in shame that he had laid the train for some outrageous
    embrace?

Absence

Love is the most mysterious of the winds that blow.
As you lie alone it batters with sleeplessness at the winter bedroom window.
The friend is absent, the streetlamp shivers desolately to and fro.
Your prostate makes you get up, you look out, police car and ambulance howl
    and flash as they matter-of-factly come and go.
There is pain and danger down there, greater than the pain you know
        But it is pain all the same
        As you breathe the absent name
Of one who is bonded to you beyond blizzards, time-zones, sickness, black stars,
    snow.

Letters

You sent a card from the Uffizi which took sixteen days to reach these shores.
A pigeon might be better, it could home in on the scaffold and count the floors.
The heart beats, I sit, I eat, I talk, I open doors
But in the everyday I am waiting for the imagined but stormily cargoed stores
Of joy and hope a letter in your upright hand tips out and restores.
        'Scrivimi!' you write.
        I do, I will, all right!
But this, though I do not send it, I give you to keep till the sun melts the rocks
    and the sea no longer roars.

Love and the Worlds

Scary is this tremulous earth, flaring, shouting, killing and being killed.
Is the universe rippling with life? What sign is there that space is filled
With anything but gas and dust and fire and rock? Are we the tillers to have it
    tilled?
I think so! And with these red hands, an act of love? Why not? We cry but we
    create, we kill but we build.
Dante was sure the stars were all – even ours – rolled out by love. They gild
        A dark that would truly scare
        If there was nothing there
The horror of there not being something, good or bad or neither, made or found,
    willed or self-willed.

The Release

The scaffolding has gone. The sky is there! hard cold high clear and blue.
Clanking poles and thudding planks were the music of a strip-down that let
    light through
At last, hammered the cage door off its hinges, banged its goodbye to the
    bantering dusty brickie crew,
Left us this rosy cliff-face telling the tentative sun it is almost as good as new.
So now that we are so scoured and open and clean, what shall we do?
        There is so much to say
        And who can delay
When some are lost and some are seen, our dearest heads, and to those and to
    these we must still answer and be true.

from TALES FROM BARON MUNCHAUSEN

My Visit to St Petersburg

Gentlemen – oh and ladies, please forgive me!
I have been too many years in the army.
But all that's in the past now. Here I am
With a gathering of my friends in this good old house.
We are cosy, are we not? Let it roar outside,
Our coals and candles, sofas, drinks replenished
Are like a magic cave where all that lacks
Is tales to tell, to startle, tales to match
The flickering shadows. My mind is full,
My memories are sharp and clear, I tell it
As it was. Judge if you will, listen you must.
Truth gives a tongue the strength of ten.
                                                    Well then,
I begin! One tingling day in December
I was skelping along towards St Petersburg
On a one-horse sledge, as they do in that country,
When a large lean cold and hungry wolf
Slunk out of the forest behind me and ran
Panting to overtake us. This was not good!
I pressed myself flat on the sledge until whoosh –
The wolf leapt over me and sank its jaws
Into my horse's hindquarters. Sorry, horse!
But that is what saved me. Now hear more.
The famished wolf went crazy, burrowing,
Munching, slurping deep into the horse
Till only its rump was showing. I rose up,
Quickly gave it the mother of all whacks
With the butt-end of my whip; the horse
Was now pure wolf, the carcass fell to the ground;
The wolf was in its harness, galloped forward
Slavering and howling till we reached St Petersburg.

247

The crowds that came out! You've no idea.
They clapped, hooted, whistled, rocked and laughed.
Great entrance to a great city, don't you think?

Frozen Music

Travelling in the wintry wastes of Europe
I found myself rattling along in a post-chaise
On a rutted road so ditched and hedged and narrow
Two carriages could never pass abreast.
One was bouncing towards me: what to do?
'Your horn! Give a warning!' I shouted to the postilion.
Well, the postilion was a sturdy lad,
Blew and blew until his lips were sore,
But nothing came out, the sounds frozen stiff
In that icy Polish air. Only one thing for it:
Necessity set my blood pumping:
I got out, hoisted the carriage on my head,
Jumped the nine-foot hedge into a field,
Jumped back onto the road beyond the carriage
That was baulked of a crash. Ha ha, I thought,
All I need now is my horses; said and done;
One round my neck, one under arm – stop kicking,
You brutes, I muttered – I got them over
By the same means, harnessed them up, drove
Laughing (and sweating just a little, I admit)
To reach the inn where we could spend the night.

That seems a fairly ordinary tale,
But there is more to come. My postilion
Hung up his post-horn on a hook by the fire,
And before you could say Pan Robinson
The music it had stored was thawed out, played

Loud and clear, untouched by human mouth,
A lovely merry medley of sweet song,
'My love is like a red red rose', 'Scots Wha Hae',
'Over the hills and far away'. I tell you
There was a tear in my eye. I called for supper
And I blessed the horn that kept its tales intact,
Letting them out, like mine, when the time is ripe.

A Good Deed

Some say Munchausen is a swashbuckler,
Too ready with a knife and gun, too wild of tongue.
Dear friends, it is not for me to defend myself.
I simply lay my life on the line before you.
It is up to you to decide. So what am I?
I was a captain in the Empress of Russia's service.
I have killed some Turks. At the Siege of Gibraltar
I helped the British. I have killed some Spaniards.
But these were wars, where 'Thou shalt not kill'
Invites derision. I have killed some animals,
Many in sport, many in self-defence:
Is that bad? I think we need a referendum!

But speaking of animals: I give you a story.
I was out hunting one summer day
Deep in the forests of Lithuania
When I saw in the distance two wild pigs
Walking in line. I shot at them, but missed,
Or almost missed. The one in front ran off,
Seemingly unharmed, but letting out a yelp.
The other one stood still – extraordinary –
Waiting patiently till I came up to her,
An old sow with her head down, silent.

I passed a hand in front of her; she was blind.
Her jaws still held a fragment of the tail
Her son had led her with. She stood helpless,
Afraid to move, yet not afraid of me,
Smell of man and smoking gun: I think
She sensed I was not now the enemy.
I grasped the piece of tail my shot had left
And led the creature, trotting docile behind me,
Back to her den.
                          Who are the cynics then?
I invented the story to appear in better light?
Did I, would I, could I help the poor beast?
I know the answer. I'm sure you do too.

Danish Incident

I wonder if you know the coast of Denmark? –
It is sometimes very cold, sometimes too hot?
I was there on the hottest day of the year,
Cantering along a fine firm stretch of sand,
Envying the waves till I could wait no longer.
I dismounted; stripped; waded out and swam,
While my horse paddled and snorted in the shallows.
I do not boast, but I am a strong swimmer,
And I made for an island well out in the bay.
Suddenly I sensed a scraping and slithering
At my legs and thighs; seaweed, I thought,
Reached down to tug it off. Wrong move that!
A head rose from the water, angry, sharp-toothed,
And the body after; I reckoned, oh, ten feet;
It was a sea-snake, and I had to think fast.
With my left hand I seized it by the neck,
With my right hand I caught it by the tail,

And then I tied it in a knot, thrust it
Squirming feebly down to the sea-bed.

So I swam on till I reached the island,
Clambered ashore. And the first thing I saw:
A clutch of baby sea-snakes behind a rock.
Even at that age they spat at me.
I admired their spirit. I am not cruel.
I left them hissing there in their stony crèche.
Some would survive to give other travellers
A useful shock. Lords of the earth are we?
Did you ever see the letters patent?
I swam back to the shore. My horse whinnied.
Only a snake, I said. He looked at me.
I got dressed, mounted, and we were on our way.

A Gibbet in Gibraltar

I was never one to scorn technology.
A strong right arm and a quick brain are vital
But sometimes more is needed. Let me tell you
About the time Gibraltar was under siege
And I was visiting some British friends there –
General Elliot, a Scotsman, better still! –
When one bright morning, neat as you like,
A shell landed on our breakfast table!
I rushed outside with it, but where to throw it?
I saw a hill with figures moving, doing what?
I took my telescope, a Dollond, best there is,
Saw Spaniards about to hang two British spies,
Too far to throw the shell, but by chance
I had with me the very sling that David
Banjaxed Goliath with – that's another story –

The sling cradled the shell and sent it straight
Into the mass of Spaniards; it killed them all,
Splintered the gibbet, freed the startled spies
Who stumbled to the sea, commandeered a boat,
Reached a British warship, told their story.

I was fêted, plied with wine, offered a commission.
But I had other lands to visit, ventures
To undertake, people unknown to make known,
The extraordinary to make ordinary.
I gave them long farewells and heartfelt thanks,
But countered any of their praise of courage
By saying 'Praise my London telescope!'

My Day Among the Cannonballs

Europe is all wars. Its plains are drenched in blood.
Treaties signed, treaties broken, forgotten,
Empires bursting from the gun of history,
Empires burnt out by the fires of history –
Should we worry, sitting here at peace?
Of course not. Yes we should. I don't know.
I know I have fought, have had allegiances,
But I am left with reminiscences,
Which are my best, least understood credentials.
Let me lay one before you. Gather round.
Come on, it's a cracker, you'll not find its like.

My company was stationed 'somewhere in Europe',
I don't remember the name of the grim town
We were besieging. It was well fortified
With gates chains embrasures machicolations
Batteries redouts vigilantes god knows what,

A bristly sort of come-and-get-me place
We had tried in vain to penetrate.
Logic, I said to myself, think logic.
We cannot infiltrate, what's left but up
Up and over, what goes up and over?
A balloon? Don't be silly, they'd shoot it down.
There's only one way, and I should emphasize
I was at the peak of my physical powers –
A long time ago, yes yes I know –
I climbed up onto our biggest cannon
And when the next huge ball began to emerge
I jumped it, like on horseback, and was off
Whizzing into the smoky air. Aha,
I thought, this is how to do it! But then,
Halfway towards the enemy, I wondered:
Would they not catch me, string me up as a spy?
Not good! I must get back, but back how?
Logic again saw just one solution:
Transfer to the next enemy cannonball
Coming towards me: a delicate operation,
But I accomplished it, and so back home.

Not the most glorious of episodes,
I hear you say. Oh but it was, it was!
Was the siege lifted? I really don't know.
Did the enemy surrender? I cannot recall.
What I remember is the exhilaration
Of the ball between my knees like a celestial horse
And the wind whistling its encouragement
And at the high point of my flight an eagle
Shrieking at the usurper of that space
Between ground and sky, between friend and foe,
Between the possible and the impossible.
I shrieked back to the wild bird in my gladness.
What an unearthly duet – but life, life!

FOR THE OPENING OF THE SCOTTISH PARLIAMENT

9 October 2004

Open the doors! Light of the day, shine in; light of the mind, shine out!
We have a building which is more than a building.
There is a commerce between inner and outer, between brightness and
        shadow, between the world and those who think about the world.
Is it not a mystery? The parts cohere, they come together like petals of a
        flower, yet they also send their tongues outward to feel and taste
        the teeming earth.
Did you want classic columns and predictable pediments? A growl of old
        Gothic grandeur? A blissfully boring box?
Not here, no thanks! No icon, no IKEA, no iceberg, but curves and
        caverns, nooks and niches, huddles and heavens, syncopations
        and surprises. Leave symmetry to the cemetery.
But bring together slate and stainless steel, black granite and grey
        granite, seasoned oak and sycamore, concrete blond and smooth
        as silk – the mix is almost alive – it breathes and beckons
        – imperial marble it is not!

Come down the Mile, into the heart of the city, past the kirk of St Giles
        and the closes and wynds of the noted ghosts of history who
        drank their claret and fell down the steep tenement stairs into
        the arms of link-boys but who wrote and talked the starry
        Enlightenment of their days –
And before them the auld makars who tickled a Scottish king's ear with
        melody and ribaldry and frank advice –
And when you are there, down there, in the midst of things, not set upon
        an hill with your nose in the air,
This is where you know your parliament should be
And this is where it is, just here.

What do the people want of the place? They want it to be filled with
        thinking persons as open and adventurous as its architecture.
A nest of fearties is what they do not want.
A symposium of procrastinators is what they do not want.
A phalanx of forelock-tuggers is what they do not want.
And perhaps above all the droopy mantra of 'it wizny me' is what they do not want.
Dear friends, dear lawgivers, dear parliamentarians, you are picking
        up a thread of pride and self-esteem that has been almost but
        not quite, oh no not quite, not ever broken or forgotten.

When you convene you will be reconvening, with a sense of not
        wholly the power, not yet wholly the power, but a good sense
        of what was once in the honour of your grasp.
All right. Forget, or don't forget, the past. Trumpets and robes are
        fine, but in the present and the future you will need something more.
What is it? We, the people, cannot tell you yet, but you will know
        about it when we do tell you.
We give you our consent to govern, don't pocket it and ride away.
We give you our deepest dearest wish to govern well, don't say we
        have no mandate to be so bold.
We give you this great building, don't let your work and hope be other
        than great when you enter and begin.
So now begin. Open the doors and begin.

AN OLD WOMAN'S BIRTHDAY

That's me ninety-four. If we are celebrating
I'll take a large Drambuie, many thanks,
and then I'll have a small one every evening
for the next six years. After that – something quick
and I'll be off. A second century doesn't entice.
When I was a girl, you thought you would live for ever.
Those endless summer twilights under the trees,
sauntering, talking, clutching a modest glass
of grampa's punch diluted to suit young ladies –
diluted? It didn't seem so! The crafty old man
loved to see us glowing, certainly not swaying
but just ever so slightly, what do you say, high.

Life put all that away. I drove an ambulance
through shells, ruins, mines, cries, blood,
frightful, days of frightfulness who could forget?
It is not to be dwelt on; we do what we can.
If this is hell, and there is no other,
we are tempered, I was tempered – fires, fires –
I was a woman then, I was not broken.
No angel either; the man I married knew that!
Well, we had our times. What are quarrels for
but to make amends, get stronger. We did, we were.
He is gone now. I don't have a budgie in a cage
but I am one, and if you want me to sing
it will take more than cuttlebone and mirror:
more than Drambuie: more than if there was ever
good news out of Iraq where my ambulance
would keep me day and night without sleep:
more than what I say here, sitting
waiting for my son to come and see me

perhaps with flowers, chocolate, a card,
oh I don't know, he is late, he is ill,
he is old, I forget his heart is worse
than mine, but still, I know he'll do his best.

You really want me to sing? Come on then,
you sing first, then a duet, I love a duet.

HORSEMEN

It was late, a wintry evening, and I was in the old flat
looking out at everything familiar, all the details
of every neighbouring house quite clear under streetlights
when at the corner by the lamp I saw them – horses and their men
talking together, their hoof clatter and whispering
(the Horseman's Word I'd read about but cannot speak),
their great flanks, fetlocks, ancient and out of place
in Glasgow now, under the streetlamp at my corner
where they should not have been.
And as I stared at them talking together all at once
every light went out and I was left in darkness with that sound
of hooves, beating, retreating –

ARRAN

It began pleasantly enough. On holiday with my parents again,
on an island in the Firth of Clyde (it might be Arran, or Milport)
meeting someone quite casually and going for a walk round the island.

Not the whole island, just going so far and then stopping
to rest in the shade. But it did not remain a pleasant affair.
This was like a Jocelyn Brooke novel (who reads him now?).

He was dark and heavy set. His corduroy trousers were hot
and red with clay dust, that man with the dog at Clambercrown,
close to the earth, and my parents elsewhere, in the background.

THE BEARSDEN SHARK

O what a whack of a black of a sleek sweet cheeky
                              tail in its big blue den
Of water! There were no bears then!
Waterworld it was, warm and salty, wet and scary,
Wild shapes, no ships, no sheep, no sheep-dip, a
                              deep deep, very!
Fish but no fishermen, no fishmen, no kingfishers, no kings,
Fish fishing for fish, yes, anglers, rays, jaws, shocks, wings,
And all those early murky milky things,
Stings on strings, things that spring.
Through shoal and shining flock and froth and freath and freaky
                              frisky flashers, like a liner,
The Bearsden shark coasts casually, kinglily, killingly
    casual, casing the scales, lazily pacing and chasing, lord
    of the place, of the plaice, lordly diner.
Little does he know of land and ocean, change and chance.
Little would he care if he knew. Little would he change if he

cared. Little would he love if he changed it. His is
reality without remorse or romance.
Heroic long-dead creature, waiting in death
To be discovered, uncovered, recovered, recalled from the cold
solid soil that never felt your breath:
We have you in a fosse, a fossil, a fragile long-forgotten
force of our growing, growling, grounded, founded but
bounding, bonding and unbonding earth.

NINE ONE WORD POEMS

A Far Cool Beautiful Thing, Vanishing
blue

The Dear Green Plaice
glasgow

Homage to Zukofsky
the

The Dilemmas of a Horn
roncesvalles

Ada Nada Paradada
dom

Lattice, Lettuce, Ladders
vasarely

Wet Dry Wet Dry Wet Asdic
dolphins

Dangerous Glory
                    morning

O Vapour-trails! O Water-melons!
                    voznesensky

FROM A NURSING HOME

– Now that you are down to one room,
Your world the room with the modest window,
Have you started thinking about it?

– About what?

– What we mentioned before.
First and last things. Don't say you've forgotten.

– I was never thinking about it.
Straitened circumstances are hardly a must.
A room is a room. As I write this
My eye sweeps round table and typewriter,
Bed and bookcase and good book-booty,
Black Marigolds, Howl, Vereshchagin,
Moby-Dick, Before Adam, Ulysses,
You Have to be Careful in the Land of the Free.
Careful, careless, carefree – we are alive
With whatever equanimity we can muster
As time bites and burns along our veins.
Wakened by gulls – god what a raucous caucus –
I wonder what makes them so angry.
Think of my shrubbery wren, I tell them,
Copy his apologetic scuttle

Among dusty late-summer leaves.
So nothing changes? Stupid anthropomorphism
Is only the idealist's last gasp.
Let the wren shriek and the gull go pitter-patter
For one surreal day, see if you like it,
I don't think so, *haecceitas* is all:
– Four Tornados have just torn the sky to ribbons
So low-flying they make my pen bounce
And my heart too for a moment. Test flights
Not in nature become so. In my room
I watch the new design emerge and shine.

IN AIR SO DEAR

Upon the middle of the day
I heard a demon sing.
You'd never guess the sweetness that
His suffering could bring.

The birds were silent, crouching low.
They knew it was not play.
They know he tries to, but he cannot
Sing the pain away.

He tries to but he cannot be
A bird in air so dear.
His clouds and darkness roll him round.
He cannot shed a tear.

But when he sings you'd think the rocks
Would break, the rivers cry.
The earth is silent. Only his throat
Trembles against the sky –

Trembles, trills, and thrills the hopes
Lying in impotence around.
Do not stop your ears before
That rending, rending sound!

RIDDLE

Up beyond the universe and back
Down to the tiniest chigger in the finger –
I outstrip the moon in brightness,
I outrun midsummer suns.
I embrace the seas and other waters,
I am fresh and green as the fields I form.
I walk under hell, I fly over the heavens.
I am the land, I am the ocean.
I claim this honour, I claim its worth.
I am what I claim. So, what is my name?

INDEX OF POEM TITLES